Taunton's **COMPLETE ILLUSTRATED** *Guide to*

Box Making

Taunton's COMPLETE ILLUSTRATED *Guide to*

Box Making

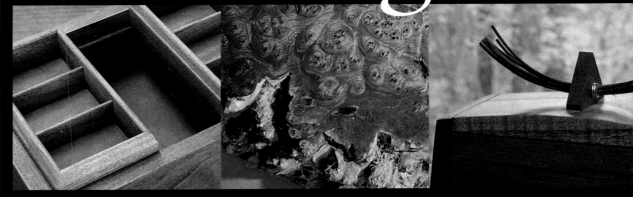

DOUG STOWE

The Taunton Press

The Taunton Press, Inc., 63 South Main Street, PO Box 5506, Newtown, CT 06470-5506
e-mail: tp@taunton.com

EDITOR: Tony O'Malley
COVER DESIGN: Lori Wendin
INTERIOR DESIGN: Lori Wendin
LAYOUT: Susan Lampe-Wilson
ILLUSTRATOR: Mario Ferro
PHOTOGRAPHER: Doug Stowe, except back cover author photo by Allen Smith.

LIBRARY OF CONGRESS CATALOGING-IN-PUBLICATION DATA

Stowe, Doug.
  Taunton's complete illustrated guide to box making / Doug Stowe.
     p. cm.
Includes index.
  ISBN-13: 978-1-56158-593-9
  ISBN-10: 1-56158-593-9
  1. Woodwork. 2. Wooden boxes. 3. Box making, I. Title.
TT200 .S7323 2004
684'.08--dc22

                    2003017442

Printed in the United States of America
10 9 8 7 6 5 4

The following manufacturers/names appearing in *Taunton's Complete Illustrated Guide to Box Making*
are trademarks: 3-M®, Bosch®, Brusso®, Incra®, Keller®, Leigh®, Lion®, Makita®, Marples®, Masonite®,
Olfa®, Omni-jig®, Stanley®, Super-Nova®, Vix®, Woodcraft®.

About Your Safety: Working with wood is inherently dangerous. Using hand or power tools improperly or ignoring safety practices can lead to permanent injury or even death. Don't try to perform operations you learn about here (or elsewhere) unless you're certain they are safe for you. If something about an operation doesn't feel right, don't do it. Look for another way. We want you to enjoy the craft, so please keep safety foremost in your mind whenever you're in the shop.

*To the students of box making. We learn from the wood,
the tools, the tradition, and each other.*

Acknowledgments

I OWE A CLEAR DEBT to box makers whose names are forgotten. Box makers who established traditions of woodworking upon which our current tools, techniques, and designs are based left unsigned legacies that inspire us still. There are living box makers as well who I wish to thank for their inspiration. Some are friends who I've met while selling my own boxes and some are box makers who have inspired me and challenged me with their published work. Woodworking is a conversation with so many participants, it becomes hard to remember who said or contributed what. I am grateful to have had the opportunity to learn from Andrew Crawford, Peter Czuk, Bill Bolstad, Michael Elkan, Terry Evans, Lorenzo Freccia, David Freedman, Michael Hamilton and Dee Roberts, James Krenov, Tom Loeser, Po Shun Leong, Peter Lloyd, Stephen Long, Tony Lydgate, Jay and Janet O'Rourke, Mark Rehmar, Jeff Seaton, Ed Wohl, and so many others omitted here, not for their lesser contribution but for the failings of my own memory. I am grateful to have gotten more than a few words and works in edgewise in such inspiring company.

With their beautiful hinges, Larry and Faye Brusso have inspired so many box makers to do better work. While I was writing this book, they retired from the business and sold the processes and production rights to a company that will carry on their work. My thanks and best wishes to Larry and Faye for playing a major part in the box-making community. I am pleased that their fine hardware will continue to be made for our use.

Woodcraft® has put catalogs of fine tools and hardware in my mailbox for more than 28 years. While I was writing this book, the company celebrated its 75th anniversary. I continue to celebrate what I have learned perusing its catalogs and I am grateful that here in a remote corner of Arkansas, I have had access to a world of tools and fine hardware.

My thanks to Tony O'Malley, my editor, for helping me to be a better writer and to Helen Albert at The Taunton Press for giving me a chance to write this book and for keeping me on track.

My wife and daughter claim I'm a different person when writing a book. I'm hard to live with and require special consideration. I thank Jean and Lucy for their support and the special consideration they provided.

Contents

Introduction · 1

Introduction

A WOODEN BOX. What could be simpler? Yet what could be more profound? Boxes have become an art form and a way in which thousands of craftsmen express themselves through wonderful works in wood. A wooden box is an expression of a complex relationship. The stuff that goes inside has had a role in inspiring the design. The material, wood, with its character, color, texture, and structural characteristics, has an age-old relationship to mankind, his culture, and his survival. To make a wooden box is to be connected to the whole of human history and to our natural environment. The pleasure we may find in making a box rests on the shoulders of our loving planet, the bounty of our forests, and the box makers who have built a tradition of caring work.

In 1865 my great-grandmother, at age 11, brought her precious possessions to the United States in a "tine" or cheese box made by an unknown craftsman in her village of Voss, Norway. It served in my mother's family as the place where family pictures were kept. Then, with its contents of photos distributed to others, the box was a part of my home as a youth, informing me of simpler days when a young man's or woman's most important things might fit in such a small space.

That this simple box could convey such meaning through more than a century tells me something important about the boxes we make. They need not be perfect to have great meaning. Make boxes for what they offer in learning. Make boxes with attention. Make boxes with love. Make boxes knowing that some may be held sacred by those you love and last generations beyond your own time.

Although this book is titled a complete illustrated guide, no book about boxes could ever be complete. The techniques used by the thousands of people making boxes could never be fully documented. In fact, it could never be complete without the inclusion of *your* work. In your box-making adventures, I ask that you experiment, make mistakes, and learn from them. Know that your work will become part of this large craft, this worldwide conversation, for future generations to discover and enjoy.

Tools for Box Making

MOST WOODWORKERS DON'T START out with ideal workshop situations. We start out with what we have, a desire to shape wood into meaningful things under challenging circumstances. I have found that great satisfaction can come from working within severe limitations. Most woodworkers dream of the perfect shop (nearly always a size larger than what we have) and crave at least one more tool. In the meantime, we can be making boxes using what we already have.

Creating Shop Space

A small shop, neatly kept, may offer feelings of intimate involvement in the work you do there. A large shop, on the other hand, may feel sterile and lonely. My current shop was designed as a two-car garage, slightly extended in length and width. Unlike most garages, however, it was designed with a vaulted ceiling to allow for long stock to be turned end for end during planing and with a dust-collector connection and electrical outlets embedded in the middle of the floor.

My woodshop occupies a slightly oversize two-car garage. The main cutting and dimensioning of stock takes place at the center of the room. Lumber is stored in racks on the wall at left. A separate finishing room prevents finishes being contaminated with dust.

A simple story stick can be made by directly measuring the intended contents of a box. Markings show height, width, and length required to contain the utensils in a silver chest. Use the story stick to set up directly stop blocks for cutting parts to width and length without ever using a measuring tool.

Measuring and Marking Tools

You can make a box without measuring at all, particularly if you make one on a lathe or bandsaw (see "Shaped Boxes" on p. 136). But most of us have become dependent on tape measures, steel rules, combination squares, and a variety of other measuring devices to bring confidence to our work. Before tape measures and folding rules became common, craftsmen used story sticks to help in the planning of work and to accurately transfer and record markings and measurements. Story sticks allow you to keep a record of the work if it is ever to be repeated. Utilizing a simple story stick to measure objects can be useful in planning a box and allows you to observe more directly the relationship between the parts of a box and its contents. It's also a good way to start the process of designing boxes.

A combination square should be one of your first purchases. You'll use it to check both square cuts and miters and to check boxes for square during assembly. I find steel rulers and other squares useful for set-ting up tools, particularly when cutting very small dimensions. I use a dial caliper to read inside and outside dimensions and mortise depths in sixty-fourths or hundredths of an inch when that level of precision is required. It may seem ironic that a craftsman would be concerned with the accuracy of the first steps, the thicknessing of wood. But the accuracy of the entire process of box making can be dependent on precise thicknessing.

To check and measure odd angles, you can use the protractor attachment for a combination square. If knowing the exact

From left to right: tape measure, 6-in. steel ruler, framing square, combination square, machinist's square, and dial caliper.

From left: a protractor head for a combination square, an adjustable protractor, an Incra rules angle guide, and a sliding T-bevel.

A variety of marking gauges (from left): an antique beech and brass gauge, a common marking gauge drilled to hold a pencil, a cross-grain marking knife, and a Marples® mortising gauge.

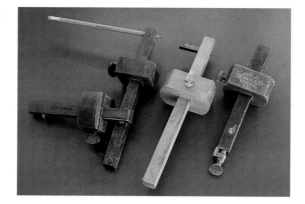

angle is not required, you can use a sliding bevel instead. It's great for laying out dovetails and transferring angles directly to the miter gauge or table-saw blade.

Marking gauges are used to lay out mortises and tenons and to establish guide marks for thicknessing stock with handplanes. They also are useful for a variety of other marking purposes. A marking gauge that I use frequently holds a pencil for marking an erasable line directly on wood.

Dimensioning Tools

Turning rough lumber into workable boards is most easily done with the combination of three woodworking tools: table saw, jointer, and planer. Many woodworkers add to this trio either a radial-arm saw or compound miter saw for easier crosscutting. The table saw is the most used tool in most woodshops. Although large cabinet saws are popular, you will find that a small contractor's saw will take up less space and be adequate for most box-making tasks. Smaller saws tend to reach their limits when resawing; this is where the additional power and blade height of a larger saw may be missed, so there is always a trade-off.

In addition to cutting stock to size, the table saw is useful for doing most joinery operations. The two most critical points in use of a table saw are your choice of blade and the alignment of the fence to the blade and miter-gauge slots. Carbide-tipped

Clockwise from top right: a stack dado blade, a sanding disk, a combination blade (on the saw), a thin-kerf crosscut blade, and a thin-kerf ripping blade.

The compound miter saw is especially useful for making repetitive crosscuts with a stop block.

blades are standard. Combination blades are particularly useful for cutting miter-key slots and very small finger joints. I use thin-kerf blades for resawing—they require less power to cut through thick stock. Because they cut more easily, thin-kerf blades improve the performance of an underpowered saw.

The compound miter saw is an excellent tool for woodworkers who have space restrictions and want to expand beyond the table saw.

The jointer and planer are the one-two punch for dimensioning wood. They work as a team—the jointer makes one face flat and the planer makes the other face flat and parallel to the first.

Although some woodworkers start projects by planing all the wood to thickness first and then cutting parts to size from the thicknessed stock, I start by cutting rough lumber into slightly oversized parts and then dimensioning them on the jointer and planer.

For space saving in my shop, I use a jointer-planer combination machine, with both tools driven by the same motor. The machine nests conveniently under one wing of my old Atlas table saw.

The plunge router (left) and laminate trimmer are adaptations of the basic router, extending the router's range of use in box making.

Not only can a bandsaw be used for resawing and stock preparation, but with a small blade it can also cut tight curves in solid wood.

When producing very small parts, I keep stock long enough to pass safely over the jointer and through the planer. I purchased a jointer long before I bought my first planer and was dependent on buying lumber already planed to thickness. But the stock wasn't always flat. If I were to do things over, and considering the inexpensive portable planers available now, I would purchase a planer first along with a jointer plane (a Stanley® #7) and a good workbench.

Shaping Tools

Many woodworking tools can help move your box making beyond straight lines and square corner joints into the more fluid realm of curves and free-form shapes.

ROUTER

The most common shaping tool is the router, which has virtually replaced most of the specialized handplanes that were once common. It can be either hand held or table mounted to cut a wide range of profiles or to be used for joinery work. The router table I use for making boxes is far simpler than

the router tables used by most woodworkers. I simply mount a router on the underside of a piece of plywood and clamp that to a workbench.

The popularity and adaptability of the basic router have led to two significant improvements that extend its range of use. The plunge router, which allows the cutter to plunge to a controlled depth into the wood, has made the router very effective for joinery work such as cutting mortises and also for removing large amounts of stock in controlled increments. The laminate trimmer, originally designed for cutting laminates for kitchen countertops, has become a popular box-making tool due to its small size and light weight, which allows you to carefully control it for delicate inlay work and hardware installation.

BANDSAW

A bandsaw is useful for resawing thick stock into thin material, but its primary purpose in most woodshops is for cutting curves. Depending on your box-making interests, a bandsaw may be either one of the most important tools in your shop or stand somewhat at the sidelines. Mine has been at the sidelines for long periods. But for woodworkers interested in free-form boxes, in making boxes on a lathe, or in working primarily with handplanes, a bandsaw would be the power tool of choice. The efficiency of a bandsaw is largely dependent on the blade. For resawing thick stock, a wide blade is preferred. Wide blades are designed to run under higher tension and are much less likely to break under heavy use. Generally, they cut straighter. For cutting free-form shapes with tight curves, a narrower blade is required.

SCROLLSAW

For cutting shapes at a tighter radius than is commonly done using a bandsaw, a scrollsaw is the tool of choice. It accepts fine blades that leave a surface requiring very little sanding. It's a great tool for doing some of the fine detail work in making pulls and feet for boxes.

LATHE

The lathe is one of the most complete tools in the shop. You can go from rough stock to the final sanding and finish of a project by using a lathe, a few turning tools, and nothing more. To hold boxes on the lathe, I use a Super Nova® chuck, which allows both the inside and outside shape to be turned without having to rechuck. For starting woodworkers with limited space and resources, a lifetime of work and growth can be accomplished on the lathe alone.

Drilling and Boring Tools

A drill press is the most accurate boring tool, with controlled depth stops and extremely accurate vertical orientation. With

You can make a turned box from start to finish on a lathe. Sand the box smooth and apply the finish while the lathe is turning and find pleasure in watching the wood come to life.

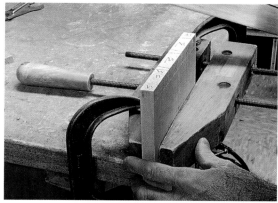

A handscrew clamped to a benchtop can be used in place of a bench vise for holding stock for handwork such as sawing dovetails.

Any vise holds work between its two jaws. A good woodworking vise also holds a workpiece on the benchtop with bench dogs.

Clockwise from right: a 4-in. by 24-in. belt sander, an inverted half-sheet pad sander, a quarter-sheet pad sander, and a 6-in. random-orbit sander. The holder for a half-sheet pad sander seems to be an invention of my own but one that has made many long hours of sanding less tiring.

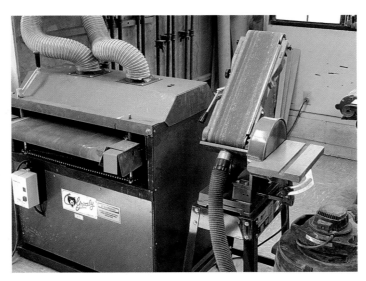

Two stationary sanders: a drum sander and a combination belt and disk sander. The belt and disk sander is more useful for box making. The drum sander is reserved for difficult woods, wide glued panels, and thick veneer stock.

a fence and stop blocks, a drill press can be an effective production tool. A hand-held drill, in contrast, can be slightly off from vertical and it has no built-in depth stop, so its accuracy is dependent on the operator.

Hand-held portable drills are common in most households and are useful in box making as well. I prefer the kind you plug in rather than cordless models, knowing that a corded one will still be at work in 20 years or more, whereas the battery-powered drill will be obsolete quickly. Additional boring tools include a dedicated mortising machine, but for small shops with limited space, a mortising attachment for the drill press may be the best option.

Holding and Clamping Tools

Woodworkers never seem to have enough clamps. You'll use them for assembling and gluing boxes and for holding parts on jigs during cutting and milling operations. They don't all do the same things effectively, so it's helpful to have a variety of types and sizes.

C-clamps are good for assembling very small boxes, but because of the amount of pressure they can exert, cushioning is required to prevent marring the wood. I use band clamps or bar clamps for assembling larger boxes. Band clamps are particularly good for assembling boxes with mitered corners. The long bar clamps and pipe clamps used in assembly of furniture feel awkward on small boxes, but I use pipe clamps when making inlay and also for gluing up wide panels from narrow stock. I frequently use handscrews or C-clamps to hold jigs, stop blocks, and router tables to the workbench. While you are waiting either to build or buy a fully equipped workbench, a handscrew held to a workbench by other clamps can serve as a temporary woodworking vise.

A workbench with a good vise and bench dogs provides an effective way to hold stock firmly while it is being planed or routed. In a sense, a well-designed workbench is the ultimate clamping device.

Sanding Tools

Sanding tools can be as simple as a block of wood with sandpaper wrapped around it, or as complicated as a wide-belt sander used in cabinet shops. I use a variety of sanding machines to make my work more efficient, such as random-orbit sanders, pad sanders, a belt and disk sander, a sanding disk in a table saw, and a drum sander. I use a drum sander to begin the sanding process when working with difficult woods like curly or bird's-eye maple or when sanding veneers to final thickness. A drum sander is not a tool that makes final sanding easier, however. It leaves coarse scratches that take some effort to remove.

I typically start the sanding process using a hand-held belt sander or a stationary belt sander, depending on the size of the box. Large boxes are difficult to hold securely on a stationary sander. In sanding small boxes, I sand through the coarse and medium grits (100 to 150 grit) on a stationary belt sander and then use a large pad sander to apply the final grits (180, 240, and 320). I use my Makita® half-sheet sander inverted in a custom-designed holder to alleviate fatigue when sanding large batches of boxes.

One of the major challenges with all the power-sanding devices available is to avoid excessively rounding over corners and edges. There are many times when a flat sheet of sandpaper clamped to the top of a work-

bench will be more effective at getting the desired results than to go through the process of machine sanding.

Hand Tools

Hand tools are either a source of frustration or a source of great pleasure, depending on whose hands they are in. I relish the opportunity to work with hand tools but have had my share of frustration in learning to use them well. Part of the challenge is in adopting the right attitude. If you have noticed children at play, they tend to give it their all without becoming overly concerned by their success or failure in the matter. That's the attitude I suggest for learning to use hand tools. When I started out with my first chisels, I was so afraid in sharpening them that I might mess

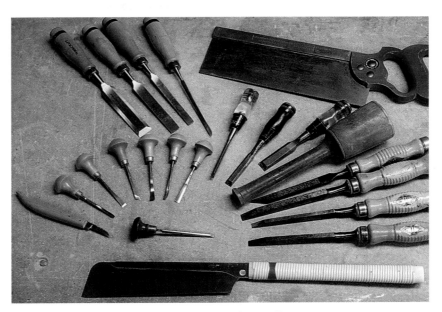

My own hand tools include English dovetail saws, German mortising chisels, commonplace carpentry chisels, small carving tools, and even a few small specialty chisels I made from old files and handles turned on a lathe.

Old planes can be bought at garage sales and fixed up for use. New wood-bodied planes are being made to match the efficiency and quality of vintage planes. Clockwise from right: a Coffin smoother by Clark and Williams, a Stanley low-angle block plane, a new Stanley block plane, and Stanley #7, #5, and #4 bench planes.

One of my favorite push-stick designs allows the hands to stay well away from the blade and enables shorter pieces to be ripped safely.

them up by getting the cutting angle wrong. I treated them as precious things rather than as tools intended to become worn out in the course of a lifetime of work. Don't be afraid to use your hand tools, to fail with them, or to sharpen them incorrectly.

I often choose hand tools over more efficient production techniques when making one-of-a-kind boxes. Essentially, most of the machine tools described so far in this section have hand-tool equivalents. A woodshop, fully equipped with all the latest power equipment, should have chisels and a few basic hand tools as well. There are times when a dozuki saw is the more practical approach than setting up a power saw to do a small task.

Noise and Dust

Noise and dust are two hazards of electric-powered woodworking. They can be a major source of irritation in a household, and they certainly endanger the health of wood-workers. It is important to use a dust mask when sanding and to collect sawdust at the point of origin during the process of cutting and shaping wood. Hearing protection should always be worn during the noisier shop operations such as power sanding, routing, and planing wood. Some tools are quiet enough to present no danger, but you should never get used to loud noises. I consider ear protection and dust collection basic requirements for power-tool woodworking. My own woodshop was designed with dust-collection ducts built into the floor, but portable units are available to make the woodworking experience much safer for the woodworker and much more pleasant for his family.

Safety and Accuracy Aids

There are several basic shop aids that can make your woodworking safer. It's worth pointing out that the same devices that make woodworking safer will make your work more accurate as well.

Push sticks, for example, keep your fingers a safe distance from the blade or bit while you push a workpiece across your saw or router table; they also help produce smoother cuts and reduced sanding. I prefer push sticks made of wood so that they can be safely cut by the blade. I make several at a time and expect them to be used up over a period of time from a variety of cuts.

Featherboards hold stock firmly against a fence or table, helping to prevent kickback. They're equally useful on a table saw and router table. Using a featherboard will help get smoother cuts and more accurately dimensioned parts.

Zero-clearance inserts prevent thin stock from slipping down into the saw. The standard blade inserts that come with table saws have wide openings designed to allow for the full range of blade tilt. A zero-clearance insert is designed to fit exactly the width of the particular sawblade being used. By giving better support to the underside of the material being cut, they also reduce splintering. Zero-clearance inserts work well on the router table, too.

Shopmade Jigs

Throughout this book, and especially in section 3 on corner joints, you'll see a variety of jigs and fixtures used in conjunction with the table saw and router table. Although you could buy most of these devices, you can make them easily with plywood and solid-

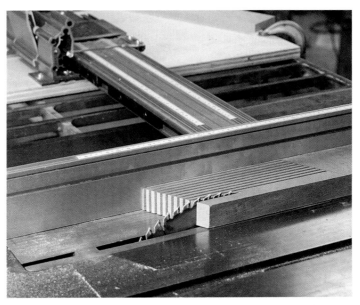

You can make your own featherboards using a table saw or bandsaw.

Zero-clearance inserts are available for many of the newer saws or can be shopmade from plywood or solid wood. The added splitter prevents stock from binding on the blade during ripping and prevents offcuts from being lifted by the back of the blade.

CROSSCUT SLED

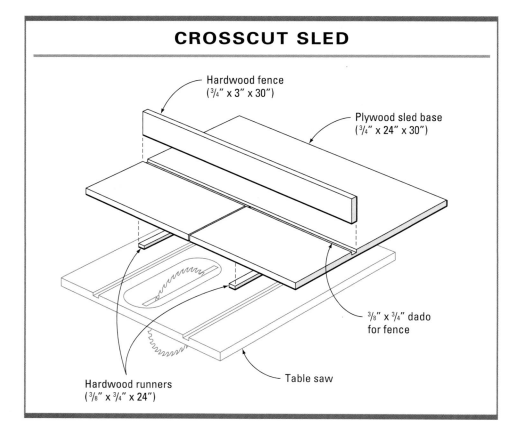

Hardwood fence
(³/₄" x 3" x 30")

Plywood sled base
(³/₄" x 24" x 30")

³/₈" x ³/₄" dado
for fence

Hardwood runners
(³/₈" x ³/₄" x 24")

Table saw

wood scraps. The drawings show the basic construction and dimensions of the ones I've made, but you can adjust both features to suit your own tools.

Crosscut Sled

A crosscut sled does the same job as a table-saw miter gauge, only a lot better. It handles larger workpieces and is permanently fixed at 90 degrees so you don't have to check the angle. In addition, a crosscut sled functions in the same manner as a zero-clearance insert, preventing chipout on the underside of the stock. When you pull the sled back from the cut, it carries both the workpiece and cut-off stock, keeping your fingers a safe distance from the blade. The fence is built-in, so you always have a place to clamp stops for repetitive cuts.

Use ³/₄-in. plywood for the sled base. Plane a pair of solid maple runners to fit in the

Zero-clearance inserts in the router table add safety to routing small parts. This insert, with an opening exactly the diameter of the cutter, is required for tenoning small parts on the router table.

miter-gauge grooves. They should fit snugly with no side-to-side play—apply a little wax to get them to slide smoothly. Attach one runner to the plywood base, square to the front and back edges. You can screw the first runner to the base from underneath. Then position the base with the attached runner in its groove and screw down through the base to attach the second runner. Make sure the screws are not too long. With the sled in position, raise the running blade up through the base as high as possible. Finally, screw a solid-wood fence to the base, making sure the fence is square to the blade.

Make a separate sled for crosscuts with the blade at a 45-degree angle for cutting end miters.

► See *"Crosscut Sled"* in use on p. 70 and p. 79.

Miter Sled

A miter crosscut sled is identical to the basic crosscut sled, except there are two fences angled at 45 degrees to the blade.

► See *"Miter Sled"* in use on p. 47 and p. 58.

Keyed Miter Sled

This sled is designed to support a box assembled with mitered corners while cutting slots through the miters. The slots are then filled with contrasting "keys" or slips of wood, which reinforce the mitered corner. Like the sled above, it's a simple plywood base with runners that ride in the miter-gauge grooves. Cut four lengths of plywood

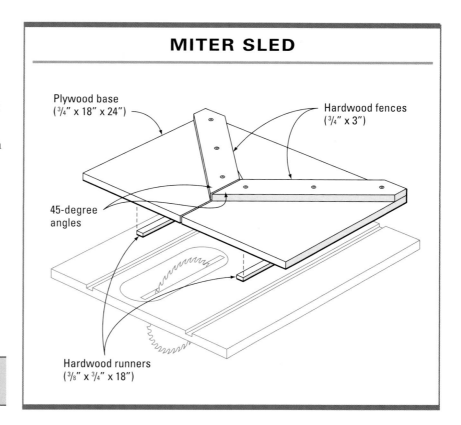

MITER SLED

Plywood base
(³/₄" x 18" x 24")

Hardwood fences
(³/₄" x 3")

45-degree angles

Hardwood runners
(³/₈" x ³/₄" x 18")

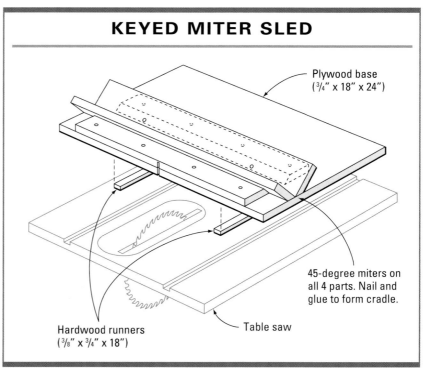

KEYED MITER SLED

Plywood base
(³/₄" x 18" x 24")

45-degree miters on all 4 parts. Nail and glue to form cradle.

Table saw

Hardwood runners
(³/₈" x ³/₄" x 18")

ROUTER TABLE MORTISING JIG

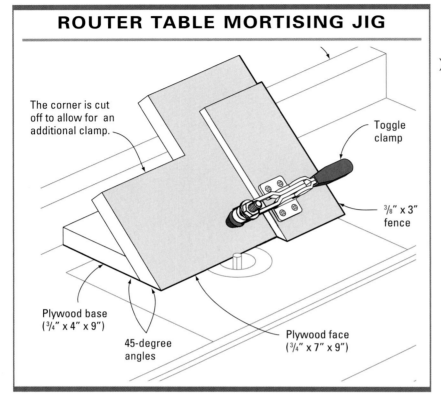

The corner is cut off to allow for an additional clamp.

Toggle clamp

$^3/_8$" x 3" fence

Plywood base ($^3/_4$" x 4" x 9")

45-degree angles

Plywood face ($^3/_4$" x 7" x 9")

TABLE-SAW TENONING JIG

$^3/_4$" x 3" x 9" fence dadoed into the face.

$^3/_4$" x 9" x 12" plywood face

Size these parts to fit around the tablesaw fence.

with 45-degree angles ripped on their edges, then attach them to the base as shown.

► See *"Keyed Miter Sled"* in use on p. 48-50.

Router Table Mortising Jig

This jig is designed to cut slots in end miters for splined miter joints. The slots can be cut through the stock for an exposed spline, or stopped for a concealed spline joint. Cut and assemble the plywood parts with mitered edges to form the jig base. I use a brad nailer and glue rather than screws to assemble the parts because it's hard to hold the parts in alignment for screwing. Attach the fence square to the working edge of the jig. I prefer a toggle clamp screwed to the base to hold the workpiece in place while making the cut, but a C-clamp will work as well.

► See *"Router Table Mortising Jig"* in use on p. 55-56 and p. 102-103.

Table-Saw Tenoning Jig

The tenoning jig rides on your table-saw fence, so be sure to carefully build the three-sided "carriage" to slide comfortably on your saw's fence. Cut a dado into the tall face panel to receive a vertical fence. Screw the fence into the dado but don't glue it; you'll need to replace it at after it's been well used.

Box-Making Materials

Rough-Milling Small Logs

➤ Milling with a Chainsaw and Bandsaw (p. 24)

Resawing Boards

➤ Resawing on the Bandsaw (p. 25)

➤ Resawing on the Table Saw (p. 26)

Working Boards with Handplanes

➤ Planing a Face (p. 27)

➤ Straightening an Edge (p. 28)

Making Wide Panels

➤ Edge-Gluing Boards (p. 28)

Making Thin Stock and Veneers

➤ Disk-Sanding Thin Stock on the Table Saw (p. 29)

➤ Making Veneers with a Drum Sander (p. 30)

MATERIALS SUCH AS METAL, glass, clay, and stone can be either cold or hot to the touch. But wood always feels just right, inviting the touch to linger. Throughout history humans have gathered wood and worked with the simplest of tools to fashion it into things of meaning and symbolic importance. Making boxes today is a link to deeply rooted elements of the human creative spirit. Wood and the love of wood have been the driving element in my own work, giving me the impulse to create.

In my years as a craftsman, I have come to view woodworking as a means of storytelling. Starting with wood, green or dry, in the log or as cut lumber, a box maker can be involved in the whole process of shaping and creating. Each box one makes is a story that tells about his understanding of tools, techniques, and materials, as well as the personal story of his growth as a craftsperson. At the same time, wood tells its own story, which starts before it falls into a box maker's hands. It's written in the grain that the maker sees and feels, begins to understand, and then retells in his own work, in the "voice" of his own experience.

Types of Wood

Softwoods, like pine and fir, come from needle-bearing trees. Hardwoods, like cherry and maple, come from leaf-bearing trees that lose their leaves in winter. Either type of wood is suitable for box making, but the hardwoods offer the greatest variety of species, colors, and textures. Hardwoods are generally associated with furniture making because of their excellent workability with either hand tools or machines. Softwoods are most often used in the building and construction trades and have historically

A walnut and pecan box with reed and brass wire. The lids are book-matched with the hole in one side matching the stain on the other. Real wood is seldom perfect but always interesting.

Manufactured wood products such as plywood, particleboard, and MDF are widely used in box making. Bending plywood (rear) can be used to create curved surfaces.

Yellow pine (top) and eastern red cedar are both softwoods. Yellow pine is harder than many other types of softwoods. Eastern red cedar is often used in box making because of its pleasant, distinctive odor. These samples are shown both natural and with boiled linseed oil finish.

been used for making bentwood boxes from wood that's still green and pliable. Exotic woods with incredible figure and grain are available from lumber dealers, allowing the box maker to bring the whole world of wood into his work.

In addition to hardwoods, softwoods, and exotics, there is now a variety of manufactured sheet goods to choose from. Wood products like medium-density fiberboard (MDF), particleboard, plywood, and others are useful in areas where their stability is an

asset to the construction of the box or to its longevity. These can be used as carcase bottoms, drawer bottoms, and substrates for veneering or for painting. Bending plywood, engineered to bend easily along one axis, can be used for boxes with curved surfaces.

Wood veneers, often as thin as $1/64$ in., are an excellent way to get the look and feel of real wood without the instability that results when solid wood expands and contracts due to changes in humidity. Veneers also are an efficient way to use highly figured woods and expensive woods to their best advantage.

Veneered plywood, already covered with the veneer of choice but on a stable substrate relatively immune to the normal expansion and contraction of solid wood, also presents some opportunity to box makers. It is often used for making top panels where the unattractive plywood edge can be hidden from view. It has been my preference to work with solid woods rather than veneers, but the use of veneers in no way lessens the quality of the work. Instead, the use of veneers may open whole new areas for creative expression.

Characteristics of Wood

Solid wood, whether hardwood or softwood, is composed of linear cells designed to carry water and nutrients to the upper branches and leaves of a tree for the production of food. This cellular structure is what gives wood its most interesting characteristics and also presents the greatest challenge to wood-workers. Because of wood's structure (imagine a huge bundle of drinking straws), wood expands and contracts in width as the cells either dry out or rehydrate from the changing moisture levels in the air. This can be a cause of frustration to beginning woodworkers. Imagine cutting some box parts to fit and then coming back the next week to put things together and finding that the parts no longer fit, are perhaps warped, or that recently assembled joints have been pushed apart by now swollen wood.

Understanding the nature of wood, how-ever, enables the box maker to plan for the inevitable, choosing joints and construction techniques that allow the natural movement of the wood to take place without disastrous consequences. The framed panel is an exam-ple of a technique specifically designed to allow for wood movement—the panel is allowed to "float" within the rigid frame.

The expansion and contraction of wood is a particular challenge because while boards expand and contract in width but not in length, the movement in width varies across different species and even within the same species depending on where a board was cut from the tree. As shown in the

Veneers present a creative opportunity for box makers, offering efficient use of rare and beautiful woods in a wide range of colors.

▶ RESPONSIBLE WOOD USE

Unlike money, wood does in fact grow on trees. But it's still a limited natural resource. There are an increasing number of programs throughout the world designed to make certain that trees are har-vested in an environmentally responsible manner. The **Certified Forest Council** is an organization that works to ensure that the woods made available by its members meet specific criteria for sound forest management and sustainable harvesting.

EXPANSION AND CONTRACTION IN BOARDS

Radial expansion/contraction occurs along a line between the center of the tree and the bark.

True quartersawn boards expand and contract the least.

Most other boards contain a combination of quartersawn and plainsawn wood. The further the board is cut from the center of the tree, the more a plainsawn board will expand and contract.

Tangential expansion/contraction follows the circumference of the tree.

wood is more valued and more expensive than plainsawn boards because there is less of it to be gotten from a tree, and the sawing techniques used to increase the yield of quartersawn lumber from a log tend to be both wasteful and time consuming. Most boards cut from a tree are part quartersawn and part plainsawn, so predicting wood movement is difficult—unless you have the time to make examining every board into a science project.

Here's the bottom line: Allow for wood movement in setting critical dimensions, prepare for movement in the design of your work, and expect movement as one of the costs and benefits of working with real wood.

Special Woods

Wood grain and color are the primary distinguishing factors that help us to identify the various species. Box makers will be interested in the special grain patterns that make their boxes uniquely beautiful. Bird's eye is normally associated with maple but can be found in cherry and other woods as well. The bird's eye is caused by an excessive number of terminal buds forming under the surface of the bark. Curly, quilted, and fiddleback grain reflect light differently from different directions, giving the wood unusual visual depth. Like many wood formations, it is not exactly clear why the bird's-eye pattern or curly figure form in wood, but there is some suspicion that the formation of a bird's eye is the result of a viral infection.

Burls are tumors that grow on the sides of some trees. Because the wood is dense and multidirectional, burls tend to be unstable, dense, and extremely rare and beautiful. Some controversy exists about their use due to the unsustainable practice of harvesting

drawing above, there are two types of wood movement—radial and tangential. Wood expands and contracts at a faster rate along the circumference of the tree (tangential) than along the radius.

Quartersawn lumber is cut with the annual rings at 90 degrees to the heart of the tree (at a true radius) and has the most uniform and lowest level of expansion and contraction. Plainsawn lumber, cut from close to the edge of the tree, will demonstrate the most movement. Quartersawn

Curly maple (top) and bird's-eye maple are prized specimens and a treasure for box making.

Burls are a rare find. This one is from a standing dead elm. Burls should not be cut from living trees because the death of the tree will often result.

The presence of the burl is visible on the outside of the tree as a growth with a multitude of bumps. The burl itself is often as beautiful as the wood beneath. The bark on this burl had been shed from the dead tree, allowing the bumpy surface to weather.

burls from living trees. The severe damage done often leaves the tree dying or endangered by serious insect damage and infestation.

Plainsawn lumber is associated with broad grain that may not be particularly "plain" in every case. In making furniture, I often find pieces of wood that don't match the grain patterns in the rest of the work. The dramatic swirls of grain may be enough to add interest to the lid of a box. Quartersawn lumber often displays ray patterns like those shown in white oak or sycamore. These patterns have a reflective quality, which makes the wood prized for box making. As an extra benefit, quartersawn woods are more stable, making them great for lids.

Another special grain characteristic prized by box makers is called spalting, which is damage done to the wood through the natural process of decay by fungus and bacteria. Spalting leaves random dark lines and areas of discoloration but also leaves areas of wood with differing densities and hardness, giving the woodworker a

Common red oak, plainsawn, has a distinctive broad grain.

When quartersawn, sycamore reveals broad ray patterns that connect between annual rings. The rays also are common in quartersawn oak.

Spalting results when fungus and bacteria mark the wood with light and dark patterns and erratic black lines. If the spalting is caught in time, the wood will remain sound when fully dried and finished.

Book-matching is a technique where wood is sawn open like one would open the pages of a book. Both "pages" will share the pattern of grain and figure, slightly affected by the loss of the saw kerf between. This sugar maple has darker heartwood, making book-matching an obvious choice for dramatic effect.

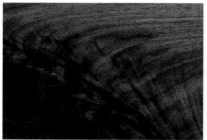

Where limbs branch from the main trunk of the tree, dense multidirectional grain forms with a radiant quality. This walnut was left over from a furniture project where the intense figure would not have been appropriate to the piece.

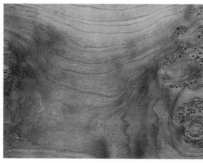

This sample of cherry shows the characteristic lighter sapwood at the top. Although all woods have sapwood, some, like cherry and walnut, are more prominent than others.

heart of the tree matures, changing color and hardness to form heartwood and giving strength to the tree. The minerals that give the heart strength give it additional color as well. Many woods such as cherry and walnut have a lighter-colored area near the bark called sapwood, which is active in moving liquid and nourishment between the roots and the leaf system. Sapwood is generally avoided in furniture making because it takes stain differently and is less resistant to decay than the heartwood. Nevertheless, interesting patterns can often be found where heartwood and softwood meet.

Matching Woods

Book-matching is a common technique that box makers use to get consistent grain and color throughout the parts of a box. In simple book-matching, a board is sawn in half through its thickness, resulting in a mirror image of grain pattern. Most commonly, book-matching is done face to face, and in

challenge in cutting and machining the wood. Spalted woods demonstrate that beauty can result from the natural process of decay in wood. When cutting and sanding spalted woods, use a dust mask to avoid possible health risks.

The areas where major limbs fork from the main trunk of the tree create interesting figure called crotch, which is at its most beautiful in walnut and is often used in making fine veneers. Other figure in wood is associated with where it grew within the trunk of a tree. As a tree matures, the inner

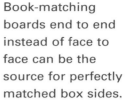
box making it is a good way to get matching woods for door panels and lids. Boards and veneers also can be matched end to end and in a variety of repeating patterns.

In veneering, the pieces are sliced rather than sawn, so the pieces will align accurately without losing wood in the saw kerf. In making veneered plywood and veneers, manufacturers commonly use a technique called slip-matching in which sections of veneers are joined sequentially but without flipping alternate pieces as in book-matching. This works well for very straight-grained woods and results in a less dramatic pattern. Normally solid woods require a great deal more experimentation and luck to make a good match. In general, straight-grained woods will give the best results. Random matching often utilizes veneers or lumber without regard to pattern or color and is used where a more rustic look is desired.

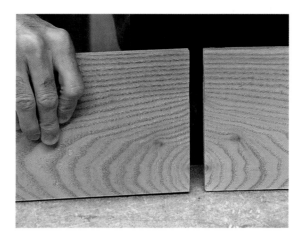

Book-matching boards end to end instead of face to face can be the source for perfectly matched box sides.

Slip-matching is a variation of book-matching. Instead of the veneer slices being opened like the pages of a book, slices are simply "slipped" side by side to form a repetitive pattern.

Jointing and Planing Wood

Moving from rough, dry lumber to materials for box making requires surfacing and squaring of the wood. This can be done with hand tools, power tools, or a combination of both. I generally use my jointer and planer to flatten and thickness stock, but it is good for beginners to learn these fundamental tasks using hand tools because they give the best understanding of the impact of wood grain on the quality of workmanship and finish. In addition, there are times when wide boards must be flattened to pass through a planer, and while many beginning woodworkers are able to afford a 12-in. planer, the high cost of an equally wide jointer is out of reach for most.

Learning to flatten stock prior to planing with the use of hand tools is a technique that will serve both amateurs and professionals. Holding a board on a workbench with a vise and bench dogs is the best approach, but smaller stock used in box making can be held for surfacing with an arrangement of clamps on a simple work surface.

I always begin the face jointing by examining the board's grain, both along the face and the edge. Using a plane on wood, you'll learn quickly that to get the smoothest cut, it is best to plane with the direction of the grain, not against it. This is true of every operation, whether done with a router, a power planer, or hand tools, but it is made most apparent when using planes. The use of handplanes is a good teacher for the kind

For those lacking a bench with a vise and bench dogs, clamps with a regular bench can serve to hold stock for leveling with handplanes.

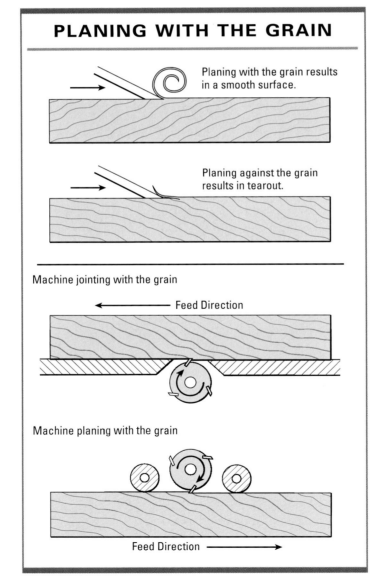

PLANING WITH THE GRAIN

Planing with the grain results in a smooth surface.

Planing against the grain results in tearout.

Machine jointing with the grain

← Feed Direction

Machine planing with the grain

Feed Direction ⟶

of careful observation that will result in better woodworking with power tools as well.

Resawing for Thin Stock

Resawing on a table saw and bandsaw are important box-making techniques. Most lumber comes in thicknesses that would be wasteful to use without resawing. In addition, resawing allows a box maker to scale materials appropriately to the size of the box. Lacking this ability, boxes would be disproportionately shaped and excessively heavy. Resawing enables you to create panels with a variety of patterns that highlight the figure of a small board in big ways.

Narrow stock can be easily and safely resawn on a table saw. You also can resaw wider stock on a table saw by cutting in from both edges of the board, turning it end for end so that the same face is always against the fence. This technique is limited by the height of the blade and the power of the saw. I use a thin-kerf blade for table-saw resawing, both because it turns less valuable wood into sawdust and also because it requires less horsepower, keeping my underpowered saw from slowing down in the cut.

Final thicknessing of thin stock can be done using handplanes on a workbench, on the planer, with a drum sander, or with a sanding disk on a table saw. Each technique has advantages and disadvantages and appropriate uses. Handplaning is the most time consuming and requires the greatest investment in learning and tool maintenance. But for those who use woodworking as an escape from the pressures of work, hand-tool use may offer the greatest sense of pleasure and satisfaction.

The thickness planer is the most efficient way to prepare wood for box making. It is noisy and requires a dust collector for regular use.

The planer is one of the noisiest tools in a woodshop, but it is extremely efficient at producing boards of uniform thickness. Thicknessing with a drum sander is a dusty operation, even with a dust collector, and is not a substitute for a planer. But for heavily figured wood, like burls, bird's-eye maple, and curly woods where grain reversals may cause tearout during planing, the drum sander is an effective solution. It is difficult to plane very thin stock. It flexes and lifts into the cutterhead of the planer as it passes through, most often destroying the wood. A drum sander can finish much thinner stock. To mill small parts for making trays and dividers, I often rip the stock on a table saw and then do the final thicknessing using a sanding disk on the table saw. The sanding disk gives a very accurate and uniform thickness.

A sanding disk in a table saw can be accurate and effective for thicknessing stock for dividers and miscellaneous parts. Only a small amount of material can be removed at a time, and the operation requires a dust collector.

I use reed, stained with dark brown fabric dye, to offer a textural contrast on small boxes. In my "winterwoods" boxes, the reed is intended to convey what it is like to touch a slender branch in winter.

This small box utilizes a rough scrap of wood found on a walk in the woods. The brass rod was polished, lacquered to stay bright, and glued into holes using epoxy glue.

Other Materials

Box making is not just about wood. Other materials provide a counterpoint to a box maker's investment in fine sanding and finish. Rough and rugged may offer a meaningful contrast to dainty and delicate. A box invites adornment with natural and man-made materials. Use of found objects can tie a box to an event or a period of time, enabling it to serve as a remembrance or as an expression your own creative spirit.

Milling with a Chainsaw and Bandsaw

A friend of mine with a tree service delivered this wood for my students to use at school. To begin milling, use a chainsaw to make the first cut down through the middle of the log. I use an arrangement of smaller logs underneath to support the log I'm cutting and to provide clearance for the chainsaw blade. A chalkline can help guide the cut (**A**). Cutting the log into rough quarters gives you two surfaces to work with on a bandsaw. It takes some skill with the chainsaw. The point here is not perfect work but merely to begin making cheap lumber (**B**). I keep the stock less than 3 ft. in length to avoid having to handle excessive weight.

Next, cut slabs off the quartered log on the bandsaw, using a roller stand to carry the weight of the log as it passes off the saw table (**C**). The bandsaw used here has a round bar that attaches to the fence for resawing stock; this allows the operator to steer the stock at the optimal cutting angle. This type of guide is particularly good for milling rough lumber on the bandsaw, since the chainsawn surface is not good enough to follow a flat fence without binding. As the log approaches the end of the cut, step around to the rear of the saw and pull it through the rest of the way (**D**). Stack and sticker the wood for drying (**E**).

Resawing on the Bandsaw

The bandsaw is an effective tool for resawing thick stock into thin stock for making boxes. Skip-tooth blades are best for resawing. A wider blade does a better job than a narrow blade, but even with a ½-in.-wide blade you can resaw 4-in.- to 5-in.-wide stock (**A**). I use blades with heat-treated teeth that stay sharp longer.

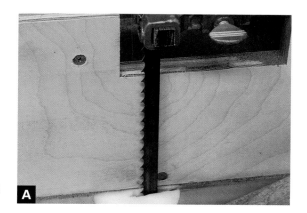

Because bandsaw blades tend to drift slightly left or right rather than stay exactly parallel to the fence, you may prefer to use a shopmade fence with a wider range of adjustment than the one that came with the saw (**B**). To adjust the fence for the inclinations of the sawblade, draw a straight line on a scrap board, and cut along the line freehand. Observe the angle at which the board has traveled relative to the fence, and clamp the fence to the same approximate angle. If the blade seems to lift the wood away from the fence and it requires effort to hold it tightly to the fence, it needs to pivot clockwise. If the wood tends to bind into the fence, pivot the fence slightly counterclockwise (**C**). Hold the stock tightly against the fence and feed it slowly into the blade (**D**).

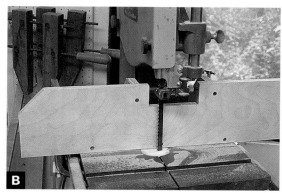

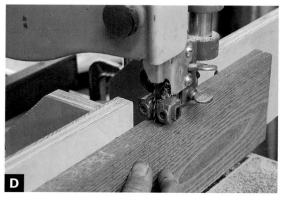

Resawing on the Table Saw

Although the bandsaw is most often my first choice for resawing a board, the table saw is a good alternative, provided certain safety provisions are made. Taking such a deep cut can be intimidating, so the operation must be done with care. It is important to start with at least one flat face and two square edges; the face will register against the fence during the cut, and each edge will ride on the table. Use a zero-clearance insert and splitter to resaw the stock. A thin-kerf blade reduces the waste and the amount of horsepower required to make the cut. This is an advantage on underpowered saws.

Clamp a featherboard to the table-saw top to give a greater degree of control and prevent kickback (**A**). Make the cut with the blade raised to the center of the stock, then turn the stock over for the next cut (**B**). Keep the same side against the fence. Resawn material can be used for book-matched panels or for matching box sides (**C**).

VARIATION To resaw boards wider than the capacity of your table saw, make two deep cuts on the table saw as shown, then finish the cut either by using a bandsaw or by hand with a common handsaw or Japanese Ryoba saw.

Planing a Face

Whether you have a jointer or planer or both, it is worthwhile knowing the basics of handplaning to flatten the face of a board. Begin by clamping the workpiece in the workbench between the vise and bench dog (**A**). If you don't have a workbench equipped with a vise and bench dogs, use a clamp and shims to hold the stock firmly in place. Use winding sticks to observe any twist in the stock. In this case, the stock has an obvious twist, which is indicated by the sticks being out of parallel (**B**). Plane the high spots and check again. I'm using a Stanley #5 plane (**C**).

When the winding sticks are parallel, you have removed the twist from the stock (**D**). Using a straightedge, check the entire surface for flatness. Here, the stock is low in the center, indicating that the ends require additional planing (**E**). Use the plane on both ends to remove the high spots (**F**).

Sometimes difficult grain will require planing from both ends to avoid tearout. When jointing a face in preparation for power planing the opposite face, a perfect finish is not required. A few rough spots will not affect overall flatness, and if you have a planer you should always plan to power-plane the hand-jointed face as well (**G**). Test as you go with the winding sticks and the straightedge. When the straightedge lies flat along the length of the stock, you're done (**H**). If you choose to flatten the second face by hand as well, follow the same steps, but you will need to gauge the thickness along the entire perimeter of the board.

Straightening an Edge

Edge-jointing is most easily done on a jointer (**A**). However, this job also can be done by hand and is far easier than a novice might imagine. A good bench vise is the best way to hold a board for jointing, but if you don't have one you can clamp the stock to the edge of your bench. Although a long plane, a #7 jointer plane for example, does the job best, you also could use a shorter bench plane (**B**). Sight down the stock to check for high and low spots. Use a square to check the angle as you go (**C**).

Edge-Gluing Boards

Often in box making it is necessary to glue wide panels from narrow stock. Well-glued joints are as strong as the wood itself but require carefully jointed edges for the glue to be effective. To give some control over the expansion and contraction of wood, I alternate grain orientation. Mark the bark side of the wood with an X and the heart side with an O to help in arranging them for gluing. I have marked the stock to show the orientation of the annual rings (**A**). Apply glue to both edges, covering them completely but sparingly. Clamp the boards together and check that the assembly is flat (**B**).

Disk-Sanding Thin Stock on the Table Saw

I often need to mill thin stock precisely for making parts for trays, drawers, and dividers for the interiors of boxes. You can mill stock accurately using a sanding disk mounted on the table saw. First, resaw the stock either on the bandsaw (see p. 25) or on the table saw (see p. 26) Using a sanding disk mounted in the table saw, sand the stock down to final dimensions. I use 120-grit self-adhesive cloth sanding material and cut a hole in the middle for the arbor (**A**). Push the stock into the opening between the sanding disk and fence, feeding it in at a comfortable rate (**B**). A sanding disk is safer than a saw blade. But using finger boards may make this operation more comfortable. Pull the stock through to complete the operation or tilt the stock up from the sanding disk at the end (**C**).

A

B

C

D

E

F

Making Veneers with a Drum Sander

It is fairly easy to make your own veneers from solid wood using a bandsaw and either a drum sander or planer. The planer will not be able to make veneers as thin as you can make with the drum sander. Although drum sanders are not the most common woodworking tool, they are effective for box making and are coming into wider use.

First, resaw your stock on a bandsaw about 1/16 in. thicker than the final thickness you want to achieve (**A**). Use an accessory fence that can be adjusted to the cutting inclinations of the blade in

▶ See *"Resawing on the Bandsaw"* on p. 25.

use. To carry the veneer through the drum sander, use a carriage board (**B**), which allows you to bring the veneer up close to the drum without damaging the feeder belt. (This same technique can be used with a planer, but the drum sander can produce veneers less than 1/16 in., whereas the planer can go no thinner than about 1/8 in.) Check the fit of the veneer slices, and adjust for the best match (**C**). Cut the veneers to approximate length and use a block plane to square and straighten the edges. I hold two pieces together and plane them at the same time (**D**). In preparing for assembly, check the fit of the planed edges. For this glue-up, I had to slide the two pieces slightly in relation to each other for the best grain alignment (**E**). The veneer pieces are too thin to clamp for gluing. Instead, use masking tape to hold the pieces together until they are ready to glue on a box (**F**).

Box Joinery

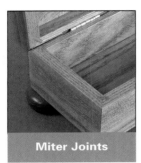

BOXES COME IN EVERY conceivable shape, including free-form and round. Most boxes, however, are rectangular and have corners that require fitting pieces of wood together with sufficient strength to endure regular use, occasional abuse, and the stress that comes from seasonal expansion and contraction. Although boxes can be made in a spirit of loose creativity, most woodworkers are interested in expressing quality craftsmanship in their work, and there is no better arena for that expression than the corners of a box.

Wood can be successfully joined with nails or screws. The nailed or screwed joint can be made stronger by adding glue. More refined joints, like the mortise and tenon, dovetail, and finger joint, can be made from wood and glue alone. A nailed or screwed joint can express coarse masculinity or spontaneity that may not be apparent in a finer joint. A dovetail or finger joint can be a statement of the maker's concerns with quality and his level of expertise. To the careful observer, beauty and purpose can be found in the wide range of corner joints used to make boxes.

Butt and Rabbet Joints

On very small boxes, a butt joint with glue may be enough to hold the joint securely for a long time. On larger boxes, butt joints require additional mechanical fastening because the repeated expansion and contrac-

This black locust recipe box was constructed using finger joints. The strong contrast between the end grain and the flat-sawn grain at the corners is both a decorative effect and a feature associated with lasting quality.

This small box of walnut and chinkapin is made with miniature mortise-and-tenon joints and dadoes to allow for a hidden drawer and bottom. The corner joints are designed to be discovered only on close inspection.

Very small boxes can be made with butt joints and glue alone and can last for a long time if they are not subjected to abuse. The smaller box on the right is only 4 in. long.

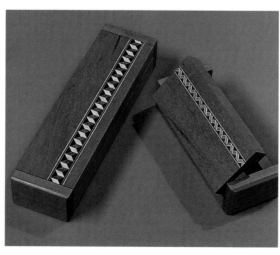

tion of the parts lead eventually to the failure of the joints. Mechanical fasteners such as nails, screws, and metal strapping provide good reinforcement for glued butt joints. Biscuits also can strengthen the joint and make assembly easier. Dowels can be used to aid assembly or can be added after the joint is glued and then sanded flush or left proud as adornment. Often the same fasteners used to strengthen the joint also speed the production, eliminating the need for clamping. Air-driven brad nails serve in this way. This technique works better for butt joints than for miters, which are hard to hold in position during nailing.

Modifications of the butt joint include the rabbet joint, which increases gluing surface area and makes accurate assembly much easier because the parts nest in relation to each other. Like the common butt joint, the rabbet joint requires additional mechanical fastening in the form of nails, screws, or metal plates on larger boxes. One big advantage of the rabbet joint over the butt joint is that dadoes for the top and bottom can be concealed in the box sides. A variation on the rabbet, the dado-and-rabbet joint, is useful in making small drawers as well. In this joint, one piece gets a deeper rabbet, forming a tongue, while the mating piece gets a dado to receive the tongue. The result is a joint that locks together mechanically and provides more glue surface than the plain rabbet joint.

Miter Joints

Miter joints are especially useful to the box maker. They are relatively easy to cut and assemble, and they allow box bottoms and tops to be fit in a concealed groove. They also allow you to use decorative inlays on

REINFORCING BUTT AND RABBET JOINTS

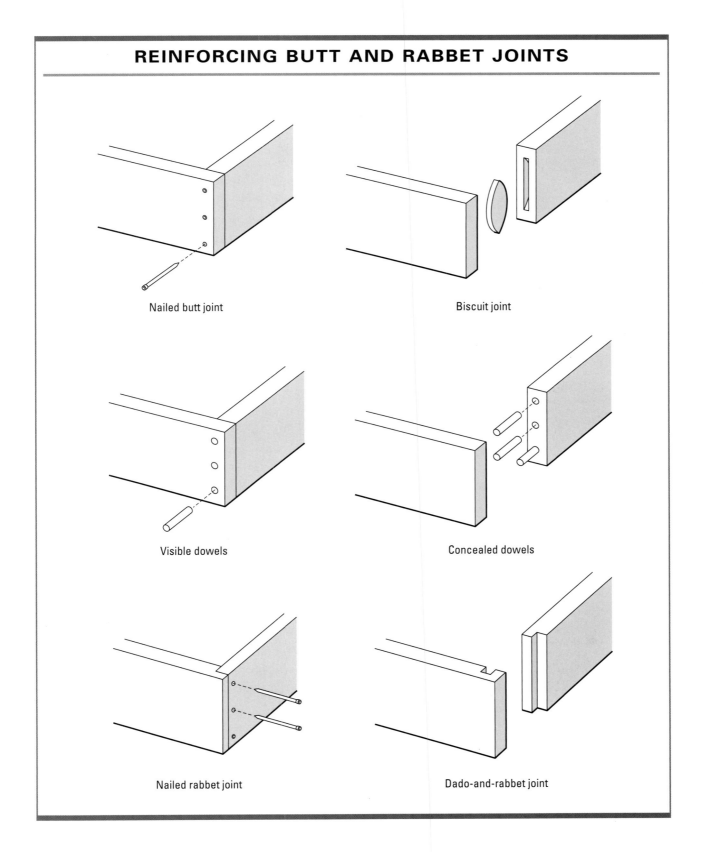

Nailed butt joint

Biscuit joint

Visible dowels

Concealed dowels

Nailed rabbet joint

Dado-and-rabbet joint

The rabbet joint increases the amount of surface area for gluing and offers some advantage over the butt joint during assembly, as the parts nest neatly together. The joint helps hide the grooves used for installing tops and bottoms.

Mitered corners allow for the use of inlay on the top edge of the box. This sassafras box with cherry and maple inlay was cut from a single board, with the grain matched to travel around the sides of the box.

This joint is excellent for making small drawers. It can be cut quickly like the rabbet joint, but the parts interlock for easier assembly and a stronger joint.

Using a combination square should be the first step in setting the angle of a miter cut. A test piece will keep you from making mistakes on the stock for fine boxes.

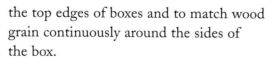

the top edges of boxes and to match wood grain continuously around the sides of the box.

I typically cut miters using a table saw with either a miter sled or an Incra miter gauge that adjusts quickly to the perfect angle. The sled allows you to cut wider stock easily but requires the table-saw arbor to be adjusted to 45 degrees. Either the miter gauge or sled will allow for the placement of stop blocks for cutting parts of uniform length. Often the corner of an assembled box may be off square, not because the angle

is wrong, but because one side of the box is longer or shorter than the one on the opposite side. Get in the habit of checking your miter cuts with a combination or machinist's square, instead of relying on the miter stops and angle indicators on your saw.

Because the grain in a miter joint is a combination of end grain and long grain, the glue bond is less than ideal. There are numerous ways to reinforce the joint, some concealed, others exposed for decorative effect. Concealed dowels, splines, or biscuits will add to the assembly challenge. Exposed slip feathers, or miter keys, are added after assembly. One of my favorite joints is the splined miter, which gives considerable strength to the joint by greatly increasing the glue area and is easily cut with a special jig on a router table.

A routed lock miter joint shares all of the good features of a regular miter, but it assembles more easily, with minimal clamping, and offers additional gluing area for a stronger corner joint. It does require a specific router bit and must be done on a router table.

Finger Joints

Finger joints are associated with fine quality in box making. Also called box joints, they became popular when wooden boxes were made as packaging for cigars.

> For more on cutting tenons on a table saw, see *"Mortise-and-Tenon Joint for Frame Lids"* on p. 78.

The quality of the cigar box was a statement of the quality of the cigars as well. Finger joints are typically cut on a router table or table saw, and a wide variety of jigs are available to make cutting finger joints more efficient. A shopmade router jig is easy to build from scrap material. With either technique, you'll want to use a backer board on the jig to prevent tearout on the back side of the stock.

To check the accuracy of a miter with a machinist's square, place two mitered pieces together and check for gaps between the wood and the blade of the square.

Whether cutting miters using the table saw or a hand miter box, using a stop block will ensure that opposite parts are exactly the same length. This is essential for tight-fitting miters.

An Incra® miter guide with a stop block clamped to the wood fence is an excellent choice for cutting smaller box sides on a table saw.

➤ CUTTING MITERS BY HAND

Many beginning box makers do not have the luxury of a woodshop where noise can be made and dust can be allowed to fly all over the room. But there are numerous hand-tool approaches to cutting miters for making boxes. Here are some of my favorites.

A shopmade miter box with a thin-kerf Japanese saw offers a low-tech approach to crisp miter joints, especially in small stock that would be dangerous to cut on a power miter saw.

First use a combination square to mark the cutline at 45 degrees.

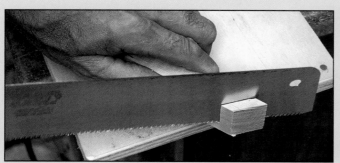

A Japanese saw works on the pull stroke, its fine teeth making it easy to hold the wood without using a vise.

A miter-frame saw quickly adjusts to a variety of angles and allows for stop blocks to be clamped in place for accurate cutting of matching sides.

A newer and more flexible tool is the Bearsaw miter guide that allows the user to cut accurate miters, square cuts, and even compound miters on wide stock. It also uses a Japanese-style pull saw.

The Lion® miter trimmer is designed to take very thin slices from stock, leaving perfect miters. It requires hand or power sawing to rough size before cutting.

Made with pau amarello and black mesquite, this box has angled slipfeathers, or keys, made from veneers and set in saw kerfs cut with an English dovetail saw. The keys give lasting strength to the miter joint and are cut and glued in after the box is glued and assembled.

On a router table, I use a spiral cutter that gives a smoother cut than a standard bit. On a table saw, be sure to use a dado or sawblade that gives a square-topped cut. For making 1/8-in. finger joints, a carbide combination blade typically offers a square-topped cut, while ripping and crosscut blades leave V-shaped kerfs that will look sloppy in the finished joint.

Mortise-and-Tenon Joints

Mortise-and-tenon joints have a great deal of strength from both the mechanical connection and the increased surface area for glue. I use a miniaturized version of the mortise-and-tenon joint for many of the small boxes I make, using the router table to cut and shape both the mortise and the matching tenon. This technique works best for very small boxes, as the cut on the router table must be a small one to do safely. For

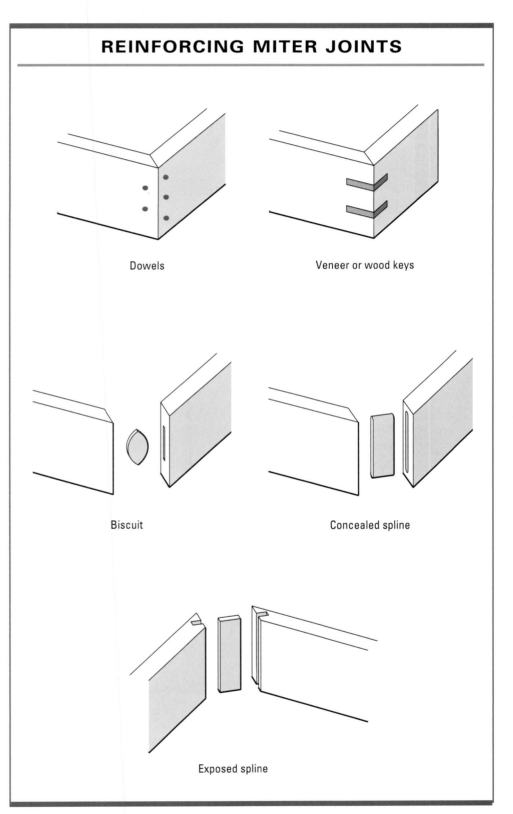

REINFORCING MITER JOINTS

Dowels

Veneer or wood keys

Biscuit

Concealed spline

Exposed spline

The splined miter is designed to give strength to the joint while being invisible from the outside of the box. The spline is revealed when the lid is cut from the base and then every time the box is opened.

The finger joint can be cut using a table saw or router. The joint is very strong due to the large amount of surface area for gluing. The visual contrast between the end grain and side grain of the wood gives a pleasing decorative effect.

A dedicated finger joint jig for the router can be made with plywood and maple runners. Use a spiral cutter for the best results.

The lock miter is a routed joint that gives the appearance of a miter from the corner view. It has interlocking fingers that give a great deal of surface area for gluing. It is an efficient production technique not often associated with finer work.

larger mortise-and-tenon corners, I prefer to cut the tenons on a table saw. Unusual in box making but beautiful and effective, through-wedged tenons offer a variation on the standard mortise-and-tenon joint.

Dovetail Joints

Dovetails are readily associated with quality woodworking. The joint is so named because the tails on one side of the joint are shaped like the tail of a dove. The mating parts are called the pins. While widely used in making furniture, they are most commonly used in making drawers where their strength is enough to handle years of regular use. They come in two common types: through dovetails, which can be seen from both sides of the joint, and half-blind dovetails, which are hidden from the front of the box or drawer. Half-blind dovetails are not a common choice for box making, but they can allow some flexibility when designing boxes that may be either carved or sculpted on the front side.

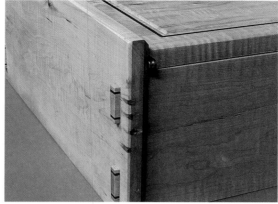

The miniature mortise and tenons used on small boxes make strong joints that are easy to assemble. A just-right fit allows the parts to be glued and assembled without clamps.

Through mortise-and-tenon joints, like these wedged with walnut, are more common to fine cabinetry but can be effectively used in box making. The wedges are glued in place after assembly.

Most people are not educated to know the difference between hand-cut and machine-cut dovetails; the differences can be subtle to the untrained eye. Learning to cut dovetails by hand has been best described as "practice, practice, practice," and the time spent using jigs is not time spent learning the finer art. The first thing a novice might notice in comparing examples of hand-cut and machine-cut dovetails is the spacing and width of the pins and tails. In many machine-cut dovetails, the pins and tails are uniformly spaced rather than arranged to fit the size and scale of the box. Very narrow pins, considered a more classic look, cannot be cut with a router due to the thickness of the router-bit shank.

Achieving the look of hand-cut dovetails has spawned a variety of jigs and devices for the router. For box makers interested in the look without quite so much effort, there also are shortcuts that speed the chiseling and sawing and make the work more accurate and less intimidating for beginners and those having less time to practice the art. Most jigs, particularly the more flexible and complicated ones, require extensive study of

These through dovetails in a sugar maple drawer were hand cut.

Routed half-blind dovetails have rounded shoulders that are hidden when the joint is assembled. The evenly spaced ones on the left were cut with an Omni-Jig. The ones on the right were cut with a Leigh jig.

the manual for setup. Less expensive dovetail jigs have a fixed arrangement of pins, sacrificing flexibility in the arrangement of pins for ease of setup and use.

I use a table saw to reduce the chore of hand-cut dovetails and reserve the use of my Leigh® dovetail jig for small production runs of boxes. On one-of-a-kind projects, I most often cut dovetails by hand. As with finger joints, mitering the top edge of a dovetailed joint can be a useful technique, allowing the top edge to look more refined and giving opportunity for inlay or carving.

The through dovetails on the left were cut with a Keller® jig. This jig sacrifices flexibility of layout for ease of use. The dovetails on the right were cut on a table saw and hand chiseled. The narrow pins are characteristic of hand-cut dovetails.

Careful arrangement of the pins and tails can be an integral part of the design process for making dovetails. These pins and tails were arranged to allow for the box lid to be cut from the base after assembly.

The Leigh dovetail jig cuts both through and half-blind dovetails with variable spacing between pins and tails. It cuts a variety of other joints as well. As with most flexible woodworking devices, there is a learning curve in its use.

The Keller dovetail jig sacrifices flexibility to ease of setup and use. A box maker will be required to adjust dimensions of work to meet the limitations of the layout of pins and tails.

LAYING OUT DOVETAILS

To cut dovetails completely by hand, you have to mark out the joint on each piece of stock. When combining machine techniques and hand-tool methods, you can get by with laying out only one of each side of the joint. But either way, good dovetails always start with the layout. Generally, I mark out and cut the dovetails, then transfer the locations of the pins directly from the dovetailed piece. I often use a pencil for the tail layouts and then change to a sharp knife when transferring the cut lines to the pin boards.

A marking gauge is used to begin laying out a dovetail joint. Set the gauge to the thickness of the stock, plus a tad for cleanup allowance.

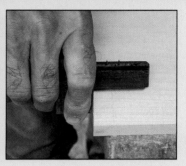

Pull the marking gauge along the end of the stock to mark the line.

Use a sliding bevel or a dedicated dovetail angle-marking jig to lay out the lines of the tails on the faces of the parts. The bevel gauge can be adjusted easily to the 1:8 ratio angle suggested for hardwoods.

Mark the ends of the tails across the ends of the boards. Note the pencil shading that indicates the waste; this helps to keep you from cutting on the wrong side of the line.

Transfer the tail layout from one board to another by laying the parts end to end.

To mark the pins, clamp a piece of scrap stock along the inside marking-gauge line of the dovetailed piece, then position the tail board over the end of the pin board. Use a sharp knife to trace along the edges of the dovetails to mark the ends of the pins.

Mark the face lines of the pin cuts with a square.

You can often clamp boxes with package tape alone or with rubber bands cut from old inner tubes. This box has hidden internal splines that help to align the parts.

When gluing mitered corners, spread glue generously on both parts. The end grain will absorb some of it.

It often takes a variety of clamps to assemble a box. Shown at the base is an old picture-frame clamp; around the center, a Merle metal-band clamp; and at the top, a cross-hatching of bar clamps.

Assembling Boxes

Different types of corner joints require slightly different approaches to assembly. Clamping is always a delicate matter, adjusting here and adding pressure there. Many of the smaller joints and the common miters in which I plan to install keys or slip feathers can be assembled with package-sealing tape and held until the glue is dry enough for the next step in the operation. Adding additional layers of tape increases the pressure on the joint. Another low-tech clamping method worth trying is to wrap large "rubber bands" cut from old inner tubes around a box.

One of my favorite joints to assemble is the routed mortise-and-tenon joint that I use on my small boxes. The tight fit of the tenons enables them to be assembled without clamping at all. Just put some glue in the mortise and press the parts together. Putting the lid in place at the same time allows you to check the box for square. Opening and closing the lid allows you to check clearance side to side.

On larger boxes, where the corner joining method becomes more complicated, clamping can become more complicated as well. In assembling a large mitered box prior to cutting the key slots, I spread glue on the end grain of each part and assemble them around the top and bottom panels. To pull the corners tight requires an array of clamps. I don't work from a formula and may do things differently each time.

Where boxes have a floating-panel top, the panel can give a quick reference for square. Observe the space around the perimeter of the panel left for expansion. You can use a framing square as well.

Another quick way to check for square is to measure both diagonals. If the box is square, the measurements will be exactly the same. If not, apply a clamp corner to corner across the longer diagonal and check again.

A floating panel gives an early indication of whether a box is square. If the gap around the panel is uniform, then the box is square.

Another quick and sure way to check for square is simply to place the box down on a flat surface and measure corner to corner from both directions. If the dimensions are the same and the box rests on the flat surface without rocking, the box is square. Whatever approach you take for assembling boxes, it's always a good idea to give the parts a test fit and watch for any difficulties. Have a variety of clamps ready to go. Slow down. If you are feeling nervous or hurried, use slower-setting glue to give yourself time to remedy any problems.

A

B

C

D

E

Nailed Butt Joint

The nailed butt joint is rarely suitable for a fine box, but it is quite effective when building a box that will be covered with veneer or painted. In this box, with angled fronts and sides, the glued and nailed butt joint makes simple work of building what would otherwise be a complicated shape. First, set the table-saw blade to 90 degrees and the miter gauge at the desired angle to give the box flared sides. (A simpler box can be made using straight 90-degree cuts.) Make the first cut with the miter gauge tilted in one direction (**A**). To make the final cuts, clamp a stop block to the fence to make certain that pairs of parts are of equal length (**B**). Spread glue on the matching surfaces sparingly (**C**). Using a board clamped to the workbench helps hold parts in position for nailing. Wax paper will prevent getting glue on the benchtop (**D**). Finally, nail the parts together; a pneumatic nail gun is handy for this (**E**).

Rabbet Joint on the Table Saw

You can use a dado blade to make rabbet cuts in one pass, but I prefer a two-cut approach that minimizes tearout. With the stock flat on the table saw, use the fence to position the first cut (**A**). Reposition the fence and change the cutting height of the blade as necessary, then stand the stock on end and make a second cut to form the rabbet. Cutting with the stock positioned between the fence and the blade gives an accurate cut and allows the waste to fall to the side (**B**). A groove cut to house the floating-panel box bottom will be hidden from view on the finished box (**C**). Assemble the box around the bottom (**D**). The rabbet joint allows small boxes to be "clamped" with plastic tape (**E**).

Dado-and-Rabbet Joint

With this joint, one side gets a rabbet cut, which forms a tongue on the end of the stock. The other side of the joint gets a dado that receives the tongue. Begin by cutting the dado using a dado blade (**A**). The distance between the fence and the outside edge of the dado cut should be equal to the thickness of the stock plus a small cleanup allowance that you'll sand away after assembly. I normally allow about ⅟₆₄ in. Next, cut a rabbet to form the tongue. Make the first cut into the face of the stock. The distance from the fence to the outside of the cut determines the length of the tongue (**B**). Make the second rabbet cut with the stock on end. This cut determines the thickness of the tongue and therefore the tightness of the joint (**C**). The finished joint assembles easily (**D**).

Cutting Miters with a Table-Saw Sled

Before using the miter sled, make certain that the sawblade is tilted to exactly 45 degrees. If the cut is always made in the same place and at the correct angle when using the sled, the sled will function as a zero-clearance device to make your cuts cleaner and more accurate. Make a cut in scrap stock and use a combination square to check for the correct 45-degree angle. Holding the stock and square up to the light will show any need for adjustment (**A**). Cut one end of the stock, then flip it over to cut the next. Using a stop block controls the length of the cut (**B**). Mark the parts as they are cut so they can be oriented with the grain running continuously around the assembled box (**C**).

➤ See *"Miter Sled"* on p. 13.

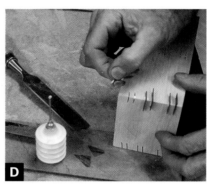

Veneer Keyed Miters

To use standard veneers for keyed miters may require some experimentation in finding the right saw. I found that my Japanese dozuki cuts too thin a kerf, but my English dovetail saw cuts one just right. As an alternate to using veneers, you can cut thin slices of stock on a table saw to the exact fit of whatever saw you choose for cutting the key slots. Make a saw guide to help direct the saw into the cut and to make the angles uniform. Clamp the guide to the box and secure the box to the bench (here one clamp does both) (**A**). Take care in your cut to stop when your saw reaches the bottom of the guide, or your key slots will vary in depth (**B**).

To make the keys, use a chisel to cut the veneer to the right size and shape (**C**). Spread glue on the key and into the saw kerf—a business card works well to distribute the glue into the kerf (**D**). After sanding and finishing, the veneer keys in this mitered box jazz up the otherwise plain corners (**E**).

Keyed Miter Joint on the Table Saw

Use a piece of scrap wood to lay out the locations of the keys in the box corners (**A**). With the stop block positioning the box on the keyed miter sled and the box carefully nested into the jig, cut the key slots. Move the stop block to reposition the box for additional cuts. The stop block clamped in place on the jig allows each key slot to be cut and still provides backing to prevent tearout during the cut (**B**).

▶ See the drawing *"Keyed Miter Sled"* on p. 13.

Rip thin stock on the table saw to fit the key slots (**C**), then use the miter gauge on the saw to cut keys to fit. I set the guide at 45 degrees to make best use of the stock (**D**). Spread glue on the keys and into the key slots (**E**). Using a dozuki saw or other thin-kerfed sawblade, trim the keys close to the body of the box prior to sanding (**F**).

[TIP] Use a combination blade for cutting the key slots. It typically has a square raker tooth between alternating bevel teeth. This gives a square-bottomed cut, which can be completely filled by the key.

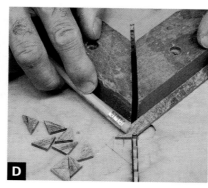

Keyed Miter Joint on a Router Table

The procedure for making this joint on a router table is exactly the same as on a table saw, shown previously, but requires a different jig made to follow a guide fence attached to the router table top. This jig is my choice for smaller boxes. A stop block placed in the trough positions the box for the first cut (**A**). The jig on the router table is designed to slide along the fence clamped in position. You could make a similar jig using a runner fitted to the miter slot made in the tops of many router tables. Slide the jig across the router bit (I use a ⅛-in. solid-carbide spiral cutter) (**B**).

To make additional cuts, turn the box around or cut the stop block shorter to change the position of the box in the jig (**C**). When cutting very small keys on the table saw, the keys can fly off dangerously in any direction. Use a small stick or pencil eraser to hold the keys in place while being cut (**D**). After the keys are glued in place, sand them flush with the sides of the box. I use a stationary belt sander tilted to a comfortable position (**E**).

Splined Miter Joint

I make this joint using a shopmade jig on a router table. On small boxes, use a ⅛-in.-dia. solid-carbide straight-cut router bit. On larger boxes with thicker sides, you can use ³⁄₁₆-in.-dia. or ¼-in.-dia. bits.

► See *"Router Table Mortising Jig"* on p. 14.

The jig travels between stops on the router table, allowing the mortises to be carefully controlled in length so as not to appear on the outside of the box. Setting up the jig on the router table requires careful measuring of the position of the stock in relation to the cutter at both ends of the range of movement between stop blocks (**A**). To accurately position the mortise in the workpiece, clamp the stock flush with the bottom edge of the jig. Place the jig and workpiece on a flat surface as you tighten the clamp, then check by feel that the edges are aligned (your fingers can feel this better than your eyes can see it).

With the workpiece clamped firmly to the jig and the jig resting against the first stop block, pivot the jig and workpiece down into the cut (**B**). Move the stock from one stop to the next and back, then lift it from the router table. Rotate the stock in the jig to rout the mortise in the other end.

(Text continues on p. 52.)

Make the tenon stock from wood equal in thickness and width to the size of the mortise. Round the edges by using a roundover bit in the router table (**C**). Carefully check the fit before cutting the splines to length (**D**). Before assembly, spread glue on the miters and inside the mortises (**E**). A well-cut splined miter can be "clamped" with package-sealing tape, but be prepared with clamps in case additional adjustment is required (**F**).

Routed Lock Miter Joint

This joint requires a specialized bit and must be used in a router table. Expect to go through some trial and error to get the right fit. Adjusting the height of the cutter to accommodate different thicknesses of stock is required. A time-saving technique is to keep a scrap from a completed project to speed the setup process. Always use scrap wood of the same thickness as the real parts to set the height of the cutter and the fence.

To make the joint, cut one piece vertically on a router table (**A**) and the other in the horizontal position. The position of the fence and height of the cutter stay the same for both cuts (**B**). Once you are satisfied with the fit, rout the parts (**C**). When routing small or narrow box parts, clamp a guide piece to ride along the top of the fence to prevent the piece from dipping into the router-table opening (**D**).

(Text continues on p. 54.)

Carefully spread glue on the surface of the joint prior to assembly and clamping (**E**). Large lock miter boxes may require clamps for gluing and assembly (**F**). Smaller joints may be effectively held with rubber bands or package-sealing tape. Stretch the tape tight before affixing it to the opposite side of the joint (**G**).

Mortise-and-Tenon Joint for Small Boxes

I cut a simple mortise-and-tenon joint on a router table using a straight 1/8-in. solid-carbide bit to rout the mortise and a larger straight bit to cut the tenon. Since the mortise is a fixed dimension determined by the size of the bit, cut the mortises first and then cut the tenons to fit. Use a dial caliper to check the depth of a sample cut (**A**). Clamp stop blocks to the fence on the router table to control the length of the cut, and slide the box end between the stops (**B**). Where an offset is required to allow for a recessed lid, use a guide piece of thin stock cut to the same dimension as the box end to facilitate setup of the opposite side.

Make the first cut in the guide piece, then flip it over end for end and use it to help reposition the stop blocks for cutting the opposite side (**C**). Reposition the fence and change the router bit to cut the rabbet that forms the tenon. This operation requires a router-table insert sized exactly to the diameter of the bit to support the workpiece safely through the cut. In this view, the safety blocking has been removed to give a clear view of the process (**D**). Move the stock from right to left between the fence and the cutter. This is a "climb feed" operation, which gives a clean cut but poses the danger of the stock being pulled into the cut. Safety blocking (as shown), a firm grip on the stock, and a sharp cutter are required (**E**).

(Text continues on p. 56.)

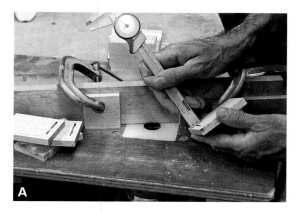

A

B

C

D

E

Check the fit of the tenon in the mortise. A perfect fit is when the tenon slips in place easily but holds enough without glue so that the joint does not fall apart due to gravity alone. Note in photo **F** that the box end has been routed for the box bottom to fit. To make the bottom fit, use the table saw to cut a groove in the box front and back. Raise the blade to the same height as the thickness of the tenon for this cut. I use a blade with a ⅛-in. kerf to closely approximate the ⅛-in. bit used to rout the mortises (**G**).

Make the shoulder cuts to finish forming the tenons. A stop block clamped to the fence of the miter gauge or sled controls the cut (**H**). Use the same setup to rout the tongues on the bottom panel. Some adjustment may be required to rout the sides of the panel due to cutting differences between the router bit used in making the mortises and the table-saw blade used to make the saw kerf in the box front and back. The climb feed, with the stock passing between the cutter and fence, gives an accurate cut, but safety blocking and a firm grip are necessary (**I**). The assembled box fits tight enough to hold together for trial fitting without glue (**J**).

Mortise-and-Tenon Joint for Large Boxes

On larger boxes, I use a plunge router to rout the mortises and a table saw to cut the tenons. Start by marking the ends of the mortises on the box parts (**A**). Set a fence on the plunge router and rout the mortises (**B**). On the table saw, first cut the tenon shoulders with the end of the stock against the fence. This cut determines the length of the tenon (**C**). It may be helpful to use some scrap stock to check the fit. With the stock standing on end along the fence, trim the tenon to thickness (**D**).

(Text continues on p. 58.)

A zero-clearance insert is required to keep the tenon from slipping into the blade slot. Check the fit of the tenon in the mortise; it should slide in without force. Cut the ends of the tenon using the miter sled on the table saw with stop blocks to position the cut (**E**). Next, cut the short tenon shoulders using the miter gauge with a fence and stop block. I do this in two steps as shown to keep chunks of wood from jamming between the blade and stop block during the cut (**F**, **G**).

Finish forming the tenon by trimming the corners with a chisel (**H**), then use a rasp to round the tenons to fit the round shape of the mortises (**I**). The finished joint will have a great deal of strength and be easy to assemble (**J**).

[**TIP**] **Whenever cutting mortise-and-tenon joints, always cut the mortises first. The cutter has a fixed width, and it is easier to fit the tenon to the mortise than to adjust the size of a mortise to an already made tenon.**

Finger Joint on the Table Saw

Making finger joints on the table saw can be done with dedicated jigs or very simply by using the miter gauge with an accessory wood fence attached, as shown here. Start by setting up a dado blade equal to the width of the fingers you want. Make a dado cut in the fence, then glue and nail a guide pin in the dado. The channel between the fingers will slip over the guide pin to position each successive cut in the workpiece (**A**).

With the miter gauge in place and the blade raised in height to the thickness of the stock (I cut a bit deeper to give a slight amount for cleanup), use a piece of stock sized to the width of the dado cut and placed between the blade and stop to position the stop block on the fence for the first cut. The Incra miter gauge allows you to easily move the accessory fence by loosening the mounting screws (**B**). A sample joint will give you the opportunity to fine-tune the fit (**C**). Slightly widen the space between the guide pin and the blade to tighten the joints. Conversely, reduce the space between the pin and the blade to loosen the fit.

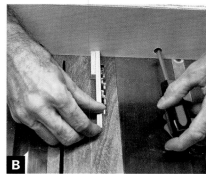

Cut the first set of matching parts using the pin as the guide (**D**). Continue to cut the fingers of the joint by moving over the guide pin for each successive cut until complete (**E**).

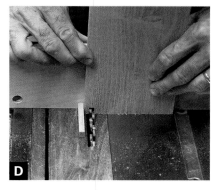

(Text continues on p. 60.)

For cutting the matching parts, make a cut using the same setup in a piece of scrap stock (**F**). Clamp the scrap piece in place and make the first shoulder cut in each of the matching parts (**G**). With the scrap piece removed, make each of the successive cuts (**H**). Continue to cut until the parts are complete (**I**). The finished joint should fit together tightly and will need minimal if any clamping during assembly (**J**).

Finger Joint on a Router Table

I use a dedicated jig to make finger joints with a router (**A**). The same technique can be adapted for use with existing router tables. In using a dedicated router jig, the procedure is the same as for the table saw shown on pp. 59–60. Make the first cuts with the stock placed against a guide pin in the fence (**B**). Next, make the same cut in a piece of scrap wood to use as the starting guide for the cuts in the matching stock (**C**).

Turning the piece over, cover the guide pin to align the next cut. Clamp the starting guide piece in place, and make the first cut on each of the matching parts (**D**). Use the guide piece only on the initial cut in each piece. Make subsequent cuts in the same manner as in cutting the first parts (**E**). These finger joints are designed to allow for the lid to hinge between the ends of the box (**F**).

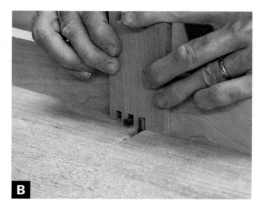

Finger Joint with Mitered Shoulder

A technique that has enhanced my appreciation of the finger joint is to miter the top edge (**A**). This permits the top edge to be inlaid and also allows boxes to be made in sizes outside the range dictated by multiples of the finger width. To make a mitered finger joint, mark the top corners of each part. Cut as usual the pair of parts that will have a solid finger at the corner. Don't cut the shoulder on the pair of parts that will have a shoulder at the top. With the rest of the fingers cut, adjust the height of the dado in the table saw to allow for a single finger thickness to remain. With the miter gauge turned to a 45-degree angle, clamp a stop block in place to position the cut (**B**). Make the matching cut by tilting the miter gauge in the opposite direction (**C**).

Dovetail Joint on the Table Saw

Lay out the joints as shown on p. 43. Using a sled on the table saw, tilt the blade to the desired angle and raise the blade height to nearly the height of the marking-gauge line. I chose the 8-degree angle often recommended for hardwoods (**A**). Change the location of the stop block and turn the stock as necessary to cut the dovetails (**B**). I chose to use narrow pins, keeping the space between the dovetails as narrow as the thin-kerf blade will allow. One consideration in this is the width of the chisel available to finish the cut.

Using a narrow chisel, clean up the space between the dovetails. Make your first cuts short of the marking-gauge line, then make final cuts with the chisel nested in the mark left by the gauge (**C**). Scrap stock clamped along the marking-gauge line helps align the tails with the pin stock when marking the pins. The guide piece allows one hand to hold the dovetailed section in place while the other marks the locations with a knife. A marking knife gives a much clearer line than a pencil (**D**). When the ends of the pins are marked, use a small square and the marking knife to extend the lines along the face side (**E**).

(Text continues on p. 64.)

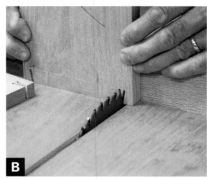

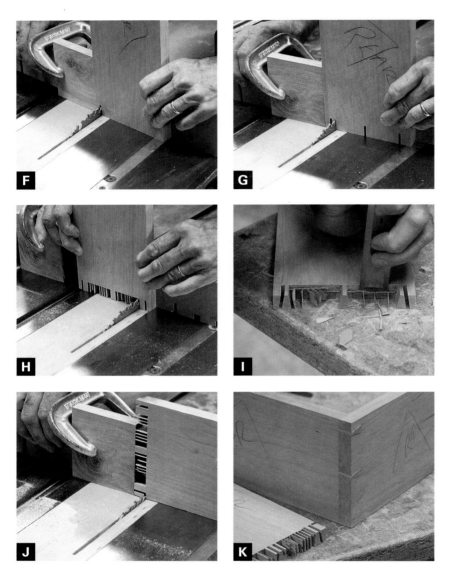

With the blade now at 90 degrees, adjust the miter gauge to an 8-degree angle (or whatever angle you cut the tails). Clamp a stop block on the fence to make the end cut on all of the pin parts (**F**). The process requires a great deal of care at this point to avoid mistakes. Cutting on the wrong side of the line is a common mistake that can be avoided by shading in pencil the areas to be removed. To cut the opposite side of each pin, change the angle of the miter gauge to the other side. Move the stop blocks as required to make new cuts, each time aligning the blade with the knife marks (**G**).

Make a series of saw cuts to remove the waste between the pins (**H**), then use a straight chisel to complete the waste removal. Make your first chisel cuts slightly away from the marking-gauge line, then finish by shearing from both sides toward the middle (**I**). Using the table saw and miter gauge with stop block, trim the outside shoulders on the pin boards. Set the saw height low enough that the piece will require removal by chisel. This will prevent chunks from becoming wedged between the blade and stop block (**J**). The finished dovetails may require some final fitting but are nearly indistinguishable from their totally hand-cut kin (**K**).

Through Dovetail with a Leigh Jig

To cut through dovetails with a jig, I have found it helpful to make the first cut with a small-diameter straight-cutting router bit. This lessens the likelihood of the bit changing depth unexpectedly when cutting dense hardwoods. The bit needs to be smaller in diameter than the narrowest part of the dovetail (**A**). After routing the straight cuts, change to the dovetail bit and rout the tails (**B**). Reposition the jig for cutting the pins, chuck a straight bit into the router, and rout the pins. When using a dovetail router jig, there is a tendency to take an overaggressive cut. Go slow and you will get a better fit with less risk of damaging the stock (**C**). Note how the pins and tails are both slightly proud of the adjacent surfaces (**D**). You can trim these with a sharp block plane or belt sander, depending on the material and the size of the box or drawer.

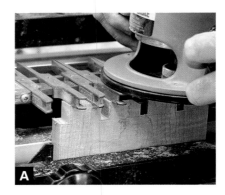

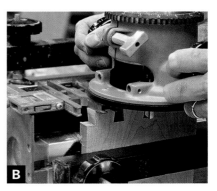

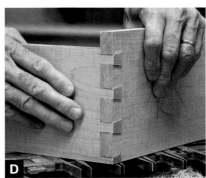

Half-Blind Dovetail with a Leigh Jig

Make the first cut with the square guide bar in place, covering the space between the fingers of the jig. As in cutting through dovetails, a light cut works best (**A**). Remove the guide bar, then rout between the fingers of the jig (**B**). Turn the routing guide over, and mount the stock horizontally for routing the pins. An accessory piece mounted in the front clamp helps to position the stock (**C**). The finished joint is clean and tight (**D**).

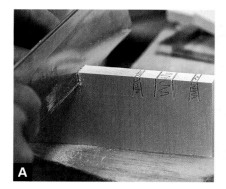
A

B

C

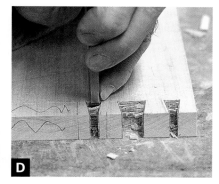
D

E

F

G

H

Hand-Cut Dovetail Joint

Hand-cut dovetails require some practice but give a sense of satisfaction in the making and a sense of mastery in the finished work. I often scribble on the areas that will be removed to help avoid sawing on the wrong side of the line. After laying out the tails, use a dozuki saw or small backsaw to cut along the marked lines (**A**).

➤ See *"Laying Out Dovetails"* on p. 41.

Once the lines are cut, begin removing the waste. Work alternately with vertical chopping cuts (**B**), followed by horizontal cuts that break the waste chip free (**C**). Here, I am using a shop-made ⅛-in. chisel. On the vertical cuts, stay slightly away from the scribed baseline. Once most of the waste has been removed, rest the chisel right on the scribed baseline to make the final cuts (**D**). Here's a little trick to help in laying out the pins: Clamp a piece of scrap stock to the backside of the scribed baseline. This allows the piece to be easily held in exact position while the pins are marked with a sharp knife.

A knife gives a more accurate line than a pencil (**E**). Use a small square to finish laying out the pins (**F**).

Using the dozuki saw or backsaw, cut as close as possible to the lines (**G**). After chiseling out most of the waste, again use the baseline to guide the final cuts (**H**). My joints always require a bit of final fitting and adjustment, so don't be discouraged if your joints don't immediately fit together perfectly.

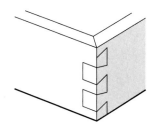

Mitered Shoulder Dovetail Joint

A mitered shoulder dovetail is simply a dovetail in which the top edge of each part is mitered instead of lapped (**A**). Lay out the parts as normal, but mark the top edges for mitering. Cutting a mitered dovetail joint is done exactly as a regular one except for the following: On the topmost pins, cut only partway through the stock, with the saw at a 45-degree angle from the corner of the box to the inside marking-gauge line (**B**). Finish the cut using the miter sled on the table saw (**C**). You could make this cut by hand using a dozuki saw or other fine-tooth crosscut saw. Make the same cut on both the pin side and the tail side of the joint. The setting of blade height is critical and must be adjusted carefully to avoid cutting into the mitered pin. Set the blade height low, and leave a bit to be cleaned up with a sharp chisel rather than run the risk of exposing the saw cut on the outside of the box. The mitered dovetail joint is a little more refined than the plain dovetail (**D**).

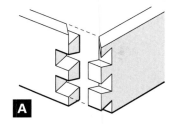

Lids

Basic Lids

➤ Simple Lift Lid (p. 73)

➤ Adding a Lip for a Lift Lid (p. 73)

Lids Cut from the Box

➤ Bandsawing a Lid from a Box (p. 74)

➤ Cutting a Lid on the Table Saw (p. 75)

Sliding Lids

➤ Dovetailed Sliding Lid (p. 76)

➤ Tongue-and-Groove Sliding Lid (p. 77)

Joints for Frame Lids

➤ Mortise-and-Tenon Joint for Frame Lids (p. 78)

➤ Bridle Joint (p. 80)

➤ Mitered Bridle Joint (p. 81)

➤ Frame-and-Panel Lids (p. 82)

THE LID OF A BOX enables you to keep personal things and very precious things from common view. Knowing this, you expect to find pleasure or surprise in the opening of lids. Then there is the fiddle factor—the strange way that manipulating objects gives a sense of power and connection, soothing the nervous soul. You watch it in the quiet clicking of ballpoint pens and, most certainly, in the opening and closing of lids.

In a sense, the lid defines your relationship to the box more than any other element of its design. Your first view of a box often comes with this question: How does it open? On many boxes, the answer is simple and quickly observed. You see the hinges on the back or the line where the lid separates from the base and perhaps the pull that directs your fingers to a point of approach. It is worthwhile to consider before starting a box how the lid will feel and work in the hands of its owner.

Lids Cut From the Box

There are two distinct approaches to making lids. One is to make the box as a closed container and then cut the lid from the box after assembly, using either a bandsaw or table saw. The obvious advantage of this method is that the alignment of the lid with the base is guaranteed. But you will have to plan the arrangement of dovetails, miter keys, and finger joints carefully to allow for the width and placement of the saw kerf.

An unfinished maple box with cherry and maple inlay. Thin cherry strips glued around the inside edge of the box form a lip that seats the lid in place.

Use a bandsaw to cut the lid from a small box in a single pass, then clean up the cut using a stationary belt sander. This box is made of black locust and mesquite.

Making the lid and box as a unit and then cutting them apart is a technique that will only work with a limited number of general box designs. To make the lid cut, I prefer to use a bandsaw on small boxes where the whole box can fit in a single pass through the saw. Larger boxes are best cut on a table saw but with the blade height set low enough so that a very small amount of stock is left to hold the lid in place during the cut. I separate the lid from the base by sliding a utility knife in the saw kerf around the perimeter of the box.

The table saw works best to cut lids from boxes that are too big for the bandsaw. Raise the blade to cut nearly through the box side, leaving a small amount to be cut with a razor knife after the sawcuts are complete.

Separate Lids

Another approach is to make the lid separately. Lids made apart from the box offer the greatest range of choices in design. They can be assembled lids or simply cut and shaped from solid wood. They can be lift lids, sliding lids, or can be hinged in a variety of ways. Section 3 shows many joints used

A white oak box with hardware handmade from steel strapping. The top is a simple solid plank that overlays the four sides of the box.

➤ FITTING LIDS

Box making requires a different level of tolerance than general woodworking or cabinetmaking, where a clearance of ⅟₁₆ in. or ⅛ in. may be close enough to look and feel right. I often put my measuring tools aside when working on lids, choosing

instead to go by feel rather than by the lines on my tools. This means more trial and error in the fitting of parts but a fit that looks and feels right.

A kitchen cabinet may require one level of fit and finish, being an item of practicality first and foremost. A box, on the other hand, is held closer to the eye and in a more intimate manner and justifies a greater level of attention.

I cut lids to size using a crosscut sled on a table saw. Use a tape measure to set the length by measuring from the sawcut in the sled to the stop block and then clamp the stop block in place. After making a trial cut of the part, check the fit in the dry-assembled box. I make the first cut the exact measurement of the opening of the box, knowing that a small amount will have to be removed for clearance.

Next, simply place the part back on the sled, and bump it over slightly from the stop block. The small amount of space between the part and the stop block will be the amount of change in length of the lid. Slide the stop block over to meet the workpiece, and clamp it in place again before making the cut. That way, if it is still too long, the procedure can be done again (and again, if necessary) to attain what you feel to be a perfect fit.

to connect the corners of boxes, and the same techniques come into play when designing and making lids. I often make lids using the traditional frame-and-panel technique found in fine cabinetry and furniture. This typically involves mortise-and-tenon joints, bridle joints, or biscuit joints on stock surrounding a floating panel designed to expand and contract with changing humidity conditions.

Solid-Wood Lids

The lid in its most simple form can be a plain piece of wood either shaped to fit a recess in the carcase of the box or shaped on its edge to fit within the box walls. After making so many complicated lids for boxes, I've found a great deal of pleasure in making a simple lid, often just a board, cut and shaped, adorned by a simple pull and allowed to rest on the top of a box. Even oddly shaped pieces may contrast nicely with a more refined base.

Solid wood expands and contracts with changes in humidity levels. On boxes, the

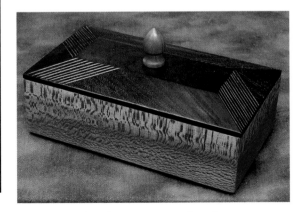

A box made of sycamore, showing quarter-sawn figure on the sides. The pull is turned from cherry, and the ebonized walnut lid is routed on the underside to fit neatly on the base. This is the simplest sort of lift lid.

outside of a lid is typically exposed to more humidity changes than the inside. This is seldom a problem on small boxes, but on

▶ See *"Box-Making Materials"* on pp. 15–23.

larger boxes where wider lids are used, some warpage may occur. One way to minimize warp is to use thicker wood because thinner woods will warp more readily. Choice of grain is another consideration. Quartersawn material is more stable than plainsawn.

On small boxes where the expansion and contraction is negligible, sliding dovetail lids work well. On larger boxes where expansion and contraction is greater, I make the lid more obviously a separate part of the box and use a rabbet and saw-kerf groove to create the sliding lid.

Frame-and-Panel Lids

Using frame-and-panel construction is the best way to ensure the integrity of the lid on a larger box. A traditional raised panel shows a small space surrounding it to accommodate expansion of the panel within the frame. I frequently use another type of panel as well, which is designed to allow for the expansion and contraction without showing the normal gap. In this design, both the panel and sides are cut using the same setting of the saw, with the tongue and groove cut on the box sides matching the same cut made in the edges of the panel. The space permitted for expansion and contraction is hidden within the joint.

In making frame-and-panel lids, the box maker has a variety of joints available. My favorite is the mortise and tenon. It has incredible strength, perhaps more than is

Sliding dovetails are a great way to make lids on very small boxes. When done well, the lids fit tight enough to give the look of a solid block of wood.

This maple box uses a tongue-and-groove sliding lid, extended at one end to allow a place for the fingers to grip.

The floating panel on this walnut box lid has a small tongue concealed in a groove in the box sides. This technique allows more uninterrupted wood to be shown on the outside of the box.

THREE TYPES OF LID CONSTRUCTION

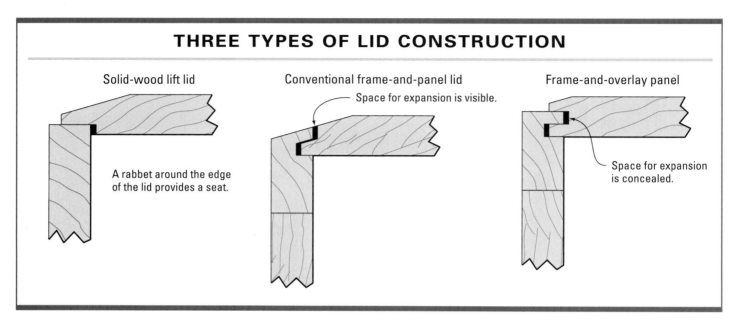

Solid-wood lift lid

A rabbet around the edge of the lid provides a seat.

Conventional frame-and-panel lid

Space for expansion is visible.

Frame-and-overlay panel

Space for expansion is concealed.

Mini biscuits are an effective way to join small box parts, especially where the size of regular biscuits would prohibit their use.

The mortise in the foreground joint was cut with a drill press and the tenon was shaped to fit the rounded mortise using a rasp. The joint at the rear was cut using a mortising machine, giving square-shouldered mortises to fit the tenons directly as cut on a table saw.

The bridle joint can be made either as a square joint or with a miter on the face side. It can be done start to finish on a table saw.

actually required for simple boxes. It is now common to use either square-shouldered tenons or rounded ones depending on the technique used to cut the mortises. A mortising machine cuts square-shouldered mortises, but drilling them on the drill press or cutting them with a router requires that either the mortises be chiseled square on the ends or that the tenons be rounded to fit. Shaping the tenons is the easier option and does little to weaken an already very strong box-making joint.

Other joints associated with better-quality work are the bridle joint and the mitered bridle joint. Both versions offer a great deal of surface area for gluing. For box makers not ready to tackle the intricacies of mortise-and-tenon or bridle joints, mini biscuit joints are a good alternative. I prefer to use double biscuits where possible.

Simple Lift Lid

Making a lift lid from solid wood requires you to cut a small recess around the perimeter of the lid to hold it securely in place when the box is closed. To do this, use a router table and fence with a straight cutter. I prefer as wide a cutter as possible for the smoothest cut; in this case I'm using a 1¼-in.-dia. bit. This is an operation where you want to make successive passes, not a single large cut, to get just the right fit. Rout the ends first (**A**). Next, rout the box sides; any tearout from the end cuts will be cleanly removed (**B**). The finished fit should have a small amount of movement side to side to allow for lid expansion but can be just a bit tighter end to end (**C**).

Adding a Lip for a Lift Lid

To make a lid that lifts easily from and sits accurately on its base, add a lip to the inside rim of the box. A simple method involves cutting a recess in the box prior to assembly and adding a strip of wood to the box side of the recess after cutting the lid from the box (**A**). My preference is to add the lip as a separate strip rather than cutting it right into the box sides. Make a router cut on the inside of the box parts prior to assembly. The depth of the cut is equal to the thickness of the lip stock being used. In this cut, I am using a ¾-in.-dia. straight-cut router bit set for a ⅛-in. deep cut (**B**).

After assembling the box and cutting the lid from it, miter-cut the strips to fit in the rabbet around the top of the box (**C**). If the lid is a bit tight, use a hard sanding block against the strips to loosen the fit (**D**).

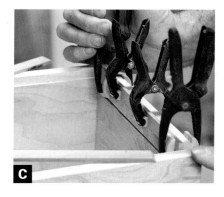

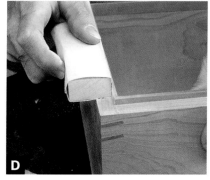

Bandsawing a Lid From a Box

My preference is to use a bandsaw on small boxes less than 6 in. or so in one dimension. This size is easy to fit under the guides of my bandsaw and also small enough so that the saw marks from bandsawing can be removed on my stationary belt sander.

To cut the box open using a bandsaw, first make certain that the blade is square to the table, that it is tracking correctly, and that the fence is adjusted to compensate for any blade drift, which is the tendency on some bandsaws for the cut to wander off a line parallel to the fence. Set the fence carefully so the cut falls where you want it. Cut the lid from the box (**A**). The edges of both the lid and the box will need smoothing to remove the saw marks (**B**). You can do this on a stationary belt sander, with a small block plane, or with a sheet of sandpaper laid on a flat surface.

Cutting a Lid on the Table Saw

I prefer to cut lids from larger boxes on the table saw. Begin by adjusting the height of the table-saw blade to just slightly less than the thickness of the box sides. The objective of height adjustment is to have enough stock left to keep the box lid from closing on the cut but thin enough that the remaining wood can be severed easily with a knife. Set the fence carefully so the cut falls exactly where you want it, then make the cut on all four sides of the box. You can test the height adjustment on the table saw by using a utility knife to probe into the first cut, but wait to score the length of the cut until all four sides have been sawn (**A**).

On this box, I have planned to have a lift lid and have made a recess around the inside of the box. Set the height of the cut to be slightly less than the thickness of the remaining stock, recording that thickness before assembling the box. Use a sharp knife or utility knife to finish the cut (**B**). When the cut is made, the lid will lift easily from the base (**C**). Smooth the sawn surface and any remaining material in the cut with a sanding block or block plane.

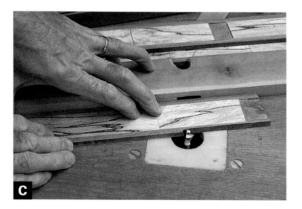

Dovetailed Sliding Lid

In making small boxes with sliding lids, begin by defining the inside shape of the box. This can be done by drilling large holes using a drill press, as I did with these boxes, or using a plunge router. I use dovetailed sliding lids on smaller boxes but plain rabbeted lids on larger ones.

> See *"Tongue-and-Groove Sliding Lid"* on the facing page.

Working with a long strip that will yield a number of boxes is safer than trying to shape very small pieces, but this technique requires that the stock be accurately dimensioned, square, and flat.

With a dovetail bit in the router table, set the fence to position the cut in the middle of the stock (**A**). The height of cut is determined by the planned thickness of the lid material. Reposition the fence to widen the trough (**B**). I turn the stock end for end to reduce the number of fence adjustments. Next, shape the edge of the lid to fit. Adjust the height of the dovetail bit in the router table, reposition the fence, and shape the edges of the sliding lid. The photo shows the operation both with and without the safety blocking in place. You can see that this operation is best done with safety blocking in place. I make this cut with the lid passed left to right between the fence and the bit for greater safety (**C**). Photo **D** shows the cut being made with a safety block over the router bit. Aim for a tight fit, then fine-tune the fit by using a block plane or sanding block.

Tongue-and-Groove Sliding Lid

On larger box lids, a sliding tongue-and-groove joint is more forgiving than a sliding dovetail. With this technique, the edges of the lid are rabbeted to form a tongue, and the tongue fits in a groove cut in the sides of the box. When building in the spring or fall, I make the lids fit to tighter tolerances, knowing that they will shrink slightly in drier months. In the winter, leave some expansion room so the lid can expand slightly during more humid weather without damaging the structure of the box.

To cut the grooves in the box sides, use a ³⁄₁₆-in. straight-cut router bit in a router table. Stop the cut shy of the end so it doesn't interfere with the adjacent end (**A**). Depending on the joinery used for the box corners, you may need to stop the grooves on two of the four sides. Position stop blocks clamped to the router table to control the length of the groove (**B**). Use a larger straight-cut router bit to cut the rabbet on the box lid. I typically begin this operation by routing a test piece of scrap wood. When you are satisfied with the fit, cut the end grain first so that any tearout will be removed when the sides are routed (**C**).

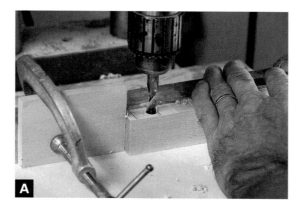

A

B

C

D

Mortise-and-Tenon Joint for Frame Lids

When cutting mortise-and-tenon joints, always cut the mortises first. Whether you plan to cut your mortises with a router, drill, chisels, or a machine mortiser, start by laying out the mortises with a marking gauge and square. You will not have to mark every piece, unless you plan to hand-chisel each mortise. Use a drill press with stop blocks to control the positions of the holes defining the mortises. Change the locations of the stop blocks to widen the mortise, leaving the stock at the middle for last (**A**). Finally, use a straight chisel to clean up the faces of the mortise. The marking-gauge lines give a perfect starting point for placing the chisel on the stock. At the bottoms of the mortises, some prying of bits and pieces will be required (**B**).

Cutting the tenons on the table saw follows a similar procedure whether using a shopmade tenoning jig or a manufactured one. I start with the deep cheek cuts. Clamp the stock vertically to the jig with the face side toward the jig body and make the first pass over the saw (**C**). Move the fence to make the second cut, keeping the face side of the stock against the jig (**D**).

For the shoulder cuts, adjust the height of the blade, and clamp a stop block on the fence to position the cuts (I'm using my tenoning jig here as the stop). Keep the stop well back from the blade so that the waste doesn't bind and kick back during the cut (**E**). Make the main shoulder cuts. As the miter gauge advances in the cut, the stop is left safely out of the way (**F**). If necessary, adjust the blade height before making the short shoulder cuts in the same way.

VARIATION 1 Small mortises can be cut on a router table, but hogging out lots of material using this technique should be avoided. Raise the router bit in small increments, and use stop blocks to control the movement of the stock and the lengths of the mortises. To reference the mortises on both ends of the stock from the face side, change the locations of the stop blocks to rout the mortise at the opposite side.

VARIATION 2 Instead of using a designated tenoning jig, use the table-saw crosscut sled and a shopmade stop block to make the deep cheek cuts on small tenons.

VARIATION 1

VARIATION 2

Bridle Joint

Bridle joints are made using the tenoning jig on a table saw. Unlike the conventional mortise-and-tenon joint, no drilling or mortising is required, so this is a good joint for beginners looking toward the next step up in the quality of their work. I typically make the tenon about one-third the thickness of the stock and set up the saw for each step by using the previously cut parts as my guide. Raise the blade to a height equal to the width of the stock plus a small cleanup allowance. I allow about $\frac{1}{32}$ in. to be sanded off after the lid is assembled and glued.

Make two cuts to form the tenon. For a tenon in the center of the stock, you can normally just flip the stock and keep the jig and fence at the same setting (**A**). Next, cut the tenon shoulders using the miter gauge (**B**). I use my shopmade tenoning jig reversed on the fence as a stop block for cutting the shoulders from the tenons. A block clamped to the fence will do as well but should be kept well back from the blade to keep the cutoffs from kicking back.

Reposition the jig to cut the mortise or slot portion of the joint (**C**). Again, you can work from both faces of the stock to minimize changes in the fence setting. Check the fit of the tenon in the slot. The slot could be cut with a dado blade, but on small boxes, I use a standard combination blade, which gives a square-topped cut and removes a $\frac{1}{8}$-in. saw kerf.

Mitered Bridle Joint

The mitered bridle joint allows the use of inlay bandings on the top of a lid and gives a cleaner look than a standard bridle joint. Cutting this joint just right can involve some careful trial and error, so I recommend that you make extra stock for a test cut and fit of the parts before cutting the finished stock.

Start by cutting the mortise or slot portion of the joint in the same manner as shown on the facing page for cutting a standard bridle joint. To make the tenon, cut the back side as you would a normal bridle joint: First make the cheek cut using a tenoning jig, then make the square shoulder cut with a miter gauge (**A**). Next, cut the face-side tenon shoulder with the miter gauge set at a 45-degree angle. Make a series of cuts to form the face of the tenon. I start with the stock up against the stop block and work my way out to finish the cut (**B**). Finally, reverse the miter gauge and cut the angled shoulder on the face of the mortised part of the joint (**C**).

Frame-and-Panel Lids

Frame-and-panel construction is one of the best ways to ensure the lasting integrity of a box lid. It allows the lid panel to expand and contract without affecting the fit of the lid on the box sides. Always cut the grooves for a floating panel first. Here I'm using a dado blade, but you could do this in more than one pass with a combination blade (**A**). In this example, the lid panel will be framed by the box sides, then cut from the box after assembly. You also can make a frame-and-panel lid as a separate assembly.

To form the panel, use a carbide blade in the table saw and make the shoulder cuts around the perimeter of the panel to begin shaping the tongue (**B**). You also can make cuts in the bottom of the panel depending on the relationship desired with the top edges of the box sides. Next, with the panel standing vertically against the fence, adjust the blade position and height to finish the cut. Use a featherboard to help hold the stock against the fence (**C**).

Cut the opposite side of the tongue by changing the position of the fence (**D**). Once the tongue is formed, you can further shape the panel on the table saw or router table. Here, I am beveling the top edge of the panel with the table-saw arbor tilted to about 8 degrees (**E**). I'll follow this cut with a sanding disk mounted in the table saw to remove the roughness left by the table-saw blade.

Box Feet and Bases

Box Feet

Box Bases

I F YOU LOOK AT BOXES from a purely practical perspective, there's really no need to add feet or a base. Often the bottom of a box is base enough. A simple routed profile can provide a line of separation between the box and the object it rests on, making it appear complete. If my purpose in the design of a box is purely functional or to express the beauty of the wood and the craftsmanship involved in its joints, I'm likely to leave it without a base or feet. Whether a box has a base may tell us something of its intended use. For example, a small box without a base may suggest that it be picked up to be used and admired. On the other hand, a base may give a box a sense of weight and the suggestion that the box only be viewed rather than held.

Handmade wooden boxes are seldom purely practical things. Although bases and feet may be regarded as unnecessary from a practical perspective, they do serve well in

This inlaid walnut box, intended as a presentation box for a gift bracelet, invites being picked up and requires no feet or base.

The turned walnut feet on this sycamore box give it an early-American feel, allowing it to fit in a more traditional setting.

A box made of highly figured bubinga with brass pegs highlighting the legs. The legs serve no practical purpose but resulted from the playful exploration of design.

giving boxes unique character, and they allow the box maker to express his own interests and personality through the design of the box. A base or feet also may be useful in making a box "fit" with other design elements in your home by echoing features associated with specific furniture styles—colonial, Art Deco, or Shaker, for example. In contemporary work, a base or feet can express humor, even reaching toward the absurd, using exaggeration or juxtaposition of divergent styles.

A trial placement of feet under a box can help you explore what you like and don't like under a particular box. Initial ideas often get modified. Here the foot at left was slightly changed to become the final foot shape at right.

Design as Play

I often use an assembled box as an opportunity to play with design. It is easy to investigate design options by placing pieces of wood underneath to form feet. I adjust them in size, shape, and position to get a feeling of how the finished box will look. Sometimes this sends me back to ground zero, making fresh parts when I discover that my original idea doesn't work. Drawings can help long before the first piece of wood is cut, but personally, I prefer playing with objects rather than the challenge of getting things drawn in perspective and scale. Often, because design for me is a process of play, the results are playful as well. Don't be afraid to stretch the limits of design in your boxes. Sometimes play is the best way to discover what you really like and may lead to something new as well.

Bases and feet tend to have different effects on the design of a box. A base may make a box seem heavier and more firmly rooted to the surface on which it rests. In comparison, feet may make a box appear lighter. So the choice whether to give a box a base or feet will be determined by the objectives of its maker.

Brass feet provide a great finishing touch for a box with traditional styling.

A box made of maple and cherry with cherry feet. The feet are assembled using the same keyed-miter technique as the corners of the box.

To further complicate things, a base may be cut or shaped in such a way as to appear lighter. In essence, the potential for the box maker to play with the design of bases and feet is without limit. For those wanting a more period look and who are not particularly interested in making feet, ready-made brass and wood feet are available. Despite the fun I have found in making bases and feet of my own design, ready-made feet are a great way to transform simple boxes to a higher level of interest and quality.

Making Wooden Feet

My tendency to use wooden feet on boxes is rooted both in being a cheapskate and in my desire to learn a wide variety of woodworking techniques. Why spend money when I can make something in my own shop that might be more interesting than something I can buy? And why spend money on something I'd enjoy learning to make myself? In addition, I've found that making my own feet allows me to adjust their scale to a size appropriate to the box I am making. Feet can be simple blocks of wood nailed, screwed, or glued to the bottom of a box. Or they can be assembled to achieve a more

dramatic and complicated shape. Feet also can be sawn directly from the sides of a box, turned on a lathe, or shaped with a router, bandsaw, carving chisels, and whatever else you may have in your tool collection.

Turning feet on a lathe is a task that requires practice and skill, both in the shaping of the wood and in being able to accurately replicate the design at least four times. This is harder than it looks, and I often make a few extra and then choose the best four as my set. Adding legs (as in the bubinga box shown on the facing page) presents a

Anything goes in the design of bases and feet. From left to right: a separate base; turned pillow feet; attached feet; and solid end panels that serve as feet.

Integral feet on these basswood boxes provide a starting point for carved or painted designs. Cut the design before the box is assembled.

A base on a larger box can house the bottom panel as well and allows for drawers to be added. In this base, the bottom panel housed in a dado helps lock the mitered parts together, serving as the primary structural element in the base. It will be screwed to the bottom of the carcase at the time of final assembly.

The rabbet cut around the inside of this cherry base provides a seat for the base. Note the matching rabbet on the bottom of the box that allows the base and box to nest tightly together.

challenge in the accurate drilling for attaching the legs with dowels. I use a simple shopmade jig to locate holes to be drilled in the corners of the box. Forming integral feet on the sides of a box can be done using a variety of techniques. My favorite method is to make a paper pattern, glue it to the wood, and cut the shape on a scrollsaw. Although a bandsaw will do the job, the scrollsaw leaves such a smooth cut that little sanding is required. Identical parts can be stacked and cut in pairs for a perfect match.

Bases for Boxes

A box base is typically a separate construction from the box itself. It may be glued and screwed to the carcase of the box, or the box might nest in the base and be secured with glue alone. By adding width and height to a box, a base can make it seem larger and more imposing. Generally, a base makes a box appear more formal than a set of feet would on the same box. In some cases, the base may provide a housing for the bottom of the box or for the addition of a drawer.

I often use add-on bases to hide secret drawers in my boxes. In any box with drawers, an add-on base allows for the mechanics of putting a bottom on the box while still providing clearance for the drawers to fit.

By shaping parts of the base prior to assembly, it can be modified to give the visual impression of feet. A scrollsaw, bandsaw, and router are all useful in making a base lighter and more attractive. I use a rabbet sawn on the inside of the base to provide a place for the carcase of the box to fit.

Integral Feet

Integral feet are cut right into the sides of the box, so you have to plan for them from the outset. Be sure to select material that is wide enough to allow for the extra height. There also is some loss of interior volume in making a box with integral feet. From a design standpoint, however, a box with integral feet offers a range of stylistic opportunities.

I often start with the sawn design and then let it influence the layout of a design for carving. This technique also works well as a starting point for traditional painting methods like Norwegian rosemaling. I cut the design directly with scissors, finding it more in tune with my style of work than a pencil and paper. Working with a folded half-template, you can cut the pattern with a matching left and right at the same time and unfold it to reveal the full design (**A**). Use spray adhesive or double-faced tape to attach the paper to the wood. Stack the parts in pairs for cutting so that left and right and front and back will be cut at the same time and be a perfect match. Double-faced tape may help if you are not confident about holding the parts together while cutting (**B**). The assembled box is ready for sanding and finishing (**C**).

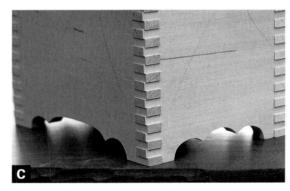

Assembled Feet

This example of assembled feet actually starts out more like making a base—by gluing and assembling the stock into a rectangular frame. You then shape the feet with table-saw cuts, producing the individual feet at the same time. Working with a frame is far easier than trying to glue up and shape individual feet. In this case, the box is made with keyed miter joints, so I use the same joinery technique to make the matching feet.

Start by gluing the mitered lengths of stock together with a frame clamp (**A**). Allow the glue to dry, then cut the slots for the keys, using the keyed miter jig on the table saw.

▶ See *"Keyed Miter Joint on the Table Saw"* on p. 49.

Glue the keys in place, then sand them flush after the glue has dried.

Make the first table-saw cut with the frame standing vertically against the fence and with the arbor of the saw tilted to the desired angle (**B**). The next set of cuts defines the footprint of the feet. Note that the sawcuts should not be made completely through the stock; leave the set of feet intact for safer handling (**C**). Cut the individual feet from the assembled frame either on a table saw or bandsaw. The last table-saw cuts trim the feet to final dimensions. Clamp stop blocks to the sled to allow the feet to be trimmed to length on both the left and right sides (**D**). Using a drill press, drill and countersink the feet for attaching to the underside of the box (**E**).

Turned Feet

Turning feet on a lathe is a pleasurable task that requires practice for good results. It is a particular challenge to make four matching feet, each with the same height and shape and with a tenon sized accurately to fit a mounting hole. I often make more feet than are required so that I can choose the best four to fit the box. I use a Super Nova chuck and cut the corners off the stock on a table saw prior to turning. The octagonal shape also gives the chuck a better grip on the turning stock and makes it easier to arrive at uniform sizes.

Begin by turning uniform cylinders, then shape the first foot (**A**). I use a variety of lathe tools to give the foot its shape and a cutoff tool to cut the tenon to size. While forming the tenon on the end of the foot, use an open-end wrench sized to match the drill bit you will use for the holes in the bottom of the box. When the wrench slips on, the tenon is the correct size (**B**). Use the first foot as a guide to marking and turning the subsequent feet. With a pen or pencil, mark the profile (**C**). Sand the feet prior to removing them from the lathe.

To install the feet, use a drill press and stop blocks to position the box for drilling (**D**). In the likely event that your feet are not exactly the same length, use a piece of sandpaper on a flat surface to slightly shorten the longer feet until the box will sit flat without rocking.

Adding Legs to a Box

A set of legs can give a box a contemporary look. They can be attached directly to the box or held at a distance for more dramatic effect. On the box shown in this sequence, I used short lengths of ³⁄₁₆-in. brass brazing rod (available from welding-supply stores) as dowels to hold the legs in place. Use a router, scrollsaw, bandsaw, lathe, or stationary belt sander to sculpt the legs to any shape you wish, but leave the shaping until after you have drilled the holes. The secret to accurate attachment of the legs is in the small drilling template.

Make the template the exact same width as the leg stock. With the table-saw blade angled to 45 degrees, cut a 90-degree V into the template block. I make the cut in from one end of the template stock and then reverse the stock for the second cut (**A**). Use the sled on the table saw with a stop block to accurately cut the feet and template all to the same length, then drill holes in the template block and all the legs at the same time so that the holes are perfectly aligned. A drill press is required. Use a stop block to precisely position each hole (**B**).

Clamp a small stop block onto the drilling template to register its position on the box. Holding it tightly in position on the corner of the box, carefully drill the holes for the brass rods to fit (**C**). I use an old carbide blade in the table saw to cut the brass rods to length (wear safety glasses to protect your eyes). A hacksaw could be used to make this cut, or wooden dowels can be substituted for the brass rods. I polish the brass rods using a polishing wheel on the drill press. Next, push the brass rods into the legs, then hammer them into place on the body of the box (**D**). A dab of epoxy glue will secure the rods, but use slower-acting epoxy to avoid rushing the assembly.

Assembled Base

This assembled base is a mitered frame glued around a plywood panel, and it functions as the bottom of the box. First, cut the end miters, then make a rip cut into the edges of the parts (**A**). Using a ⅛-in.-thick Baltic birch plywood bottom requires only a single cut on each piece. Thicker material for the bottom would require a second pass.

Cut about halfway through the width of the stock for a good strong bottom. Before assembly, sand the inside edges. Glue the parts together, with glue on the mitered surfaces and inside the grooves so that the plywood is secured on all edges (**B**). Clamp the assembled base while the glue dries (**C**). You can do additional shaping to the outside of the base after assembly. Use screws to attach the base to the bottom edges of the box sides (**D**).

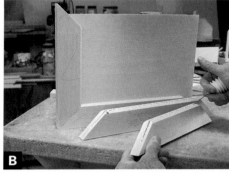

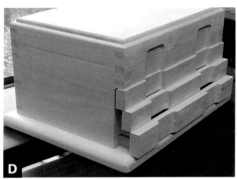

Routed Frame Base

To make a small routed base for a box, I start giving the base its shape before cutting the parts to finished length. Using a router table with a straight-cut bit, shape the base stock. Use a stop block on the router table to control the movement of the stock along the fence (**A**). Because there can be some severe tearout during this operation, make the cut in small increments and cut from the right to the left, stopping well short of the end of the cut. Flip the stock over to cut the opposite side of the piece. You'll need to change the position of stop blocks to cut a similar pattern in the shorter stock for the sides. You can make the base as elaborate as you wish with a variety of cuts (**B**). Cut a rabbet in the top edge of the parts as a ledge for the box to rest on. Miter the ends of the stock and assemble the base (**C**).

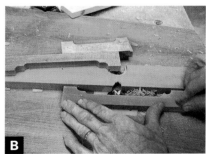

Secret Drawer Base

A base makes a great hiding place for a secret drawer. I make secret drawer bases to attach on the underside of some of my production boxes. Three sides of the base are firmly attached to the box; the fourth side becomes the drawer front attached to a separate drawer box. In this example, pieces of ⅛-in.-thick Baltic birch plywood serve as the bottom of the box and the drawer bottom (the pieces are exactly the same size). In addition, the drawer bottom extends past the edge of the sides, forming drawer runners that slide in grooves in the sides of the base.

First, cut the base parts to length with mitered ends, then cut grooves into the inside edges of the parts on the table saw. A single pass should do it, but make sure the kerf isn't too tight or loose for the bottom material. All four pieces get two grooves (**A**). Spread glue in the top saw kerfs where the box bottom fits, being careful not to put glue into the saw kerf on the drawer front. This essentially glues the box bottom on three sides (**B**). Use a band clamp to hold the parts together for gluing (**C**). Glue the drawer bottom to the drawer front.

To form the drawer sides on the secret drawer, glue pieces of wood directly to the drawer bottom, leaving clearance on the sides for the drawer to fit within the sides of the base (**D**). Shape the edges of the base before sanding and attaching the base unit to the finished box (**E**). Use construction adhesive to attach the base to the box, and use either package-sealing tape or masking tape to secure the pieces while the adhesive dries (**F**).

Box Interiors

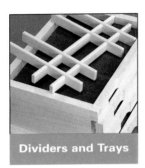

Dividers and Trays

Drawers

Box Linings

OUTFITTING THE INSIDE of a box is no less challenging than making the outside. A box with interior components can be more complex than a large piece of furniture. There may be trays that lift or slide. Perhaps dividers, drawers, doors, hangers, and other fittings are involved. Each of these features adds usefulness to the box, particularly for safely holding the small things that require some organization and special care. Jewelry boxes are among the most challenging and complicated of boxes and require the most planning and fore-thought. Parts that fit and move within the confines of a box demand a high level of precision and can challenge even experi-enced craftsmen.

These interior parts are what turn an empty box into an efficient storage device and sometimes an engineering marvel as well. On the other side of the equation is the often-overlooked maxim: "Keep it simple!" Inherent in complexity is the possibility of making mistakes. So, when making a complicated box, you are faced with the challenge: How can you make it as simply as possible?

Making Models and Mock-Ups

Although many simple boxes can be made with little planning, when I make a more complicated box, I often make a simple model of the whole box or mock-ups of the working parts. Models and mock-ups help

> **THREE RULES FOR KEEPING IT SIMPLE**

You don't need to reinvent the wheel every time you make a box, and if you are a beginner, don't try to learn everything on your first project. Things have a tendency to get complicated. And even as an advanced woodworker, I try to apply these three rules to minimize complications and errors.

1. Make full-scale drawings or physical mock-ups of moving parts. For most small boxes, making full-scale models or drawings is much easier than when making furniture, and they will help you anticipate problems in the design.

2. Use the same joinery techniques for both the outside of the box and its inside components. This will keep the learning curve manageable and allow you to be better practiced in the technique.

3. Carefully plan the sequence of operations. It is easy to get ahead of yourself, making cuts that would best be made on an assembled piece rather than on small parts, or conversely, forgetting to make cuts until after parts are assembled when they are more difficult to make accurately.

me resolve design issues and gain a better understanding of the relationship between moving parts than I would get from a drawing alone. For instance, when making a hinged lift tray inside a jewelry box, I mock up the parts in thin plywood or particleboard. This allows me to observe the parts through their full range of motion.

Interior Joinery

Fortunately, the interior parts of boxes can be made using many of the same techniques used for making the exterior. The full range of joinery techniques, from keyed miters to dovetails, are useful for making doors, trays, compartments, and drawers. I often use the same technique for both the corners of the box and for the corners of the tray that fits inside. This provides visual and design continuity between the inside and the outside of the box.

It's worth asking the question, however: "Do I want the inside of the box to reflect the outside or to bring surprises?" Often, in making a dovetailed box, I'll use a simpler mortise-and-tenon drawer, both to make the work easier and because the scale of the drawer is such that the simpler technique will be sufficient in strength. Or I may choose instead to go for broke on the inside of a box, using finer techniques like hand-cut dovetails to enhance the interior design.

Planning the Sequence

Developing an understanding of the best sequence for milling parts and cutting joints is a challenge for all woodworkers. As you gain experience in making boxes, some things will become more obvious. For instance, the jewelry chest sides shown in

A jewelry box can have doors and drawers in addition to its lid, making it as complicated as a large piece of furniture, only on a much smaller scale.

the photo above are constructed as a mitered frame held together with mini biscuits. Each houses a floating panel. It makes sense to drill the necklace hangers before assembly and to rout for drawer guides after the sides are assembled as larger units. The primary consideration in this specific case is that the part that is drilled for the hangers is a floating panel and would be difficult to

Here's the simple mock-up of a hinged lid and tray assembly next to the finished box it was designed for. The mock-up provided the exact dimensions for the interior parts and the precise location for mounting the hardware.

This is a small cabinet for jewelry with fabric wings for pins and earrings and dovetailed drawers. Sometimes the interior can bring surprises.

hold securely for accurate drilling after assembly. The fitting of the drawer guides, on the other hand, would be a serious challenge to accomplish on loose parts prior to being assembled into larger units.

A simple guideline to follow in developing a sequence for shaping parts is this: If it can be done most accurately on a small part prior to assembly, do it first. Otherwise, wait until the parts are assembled and easier to handle as a unit.

Drawers

Some of the boxes I make are small chests of drawers. Drawers are a great way to add highly organized space to the interior of a box. You can add drawers within the base of a box, or you can design the box itself to allow the addition of drawers within its

Routing slots for these drawer guides would be difficult before assembly of the frame-and-panel sides, so wait until the side frame is assembled for easier and more accurate milling.

Half-lapped dividers can be assembled as a unit and added to drawers, trays, and the carcase of a box.

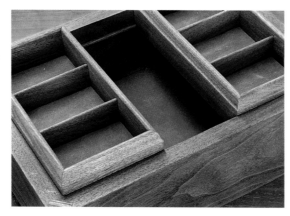

Sliding trays can fit on a simple runner recessed into the sides of a box. They are a great way to make use of depth in a box and can be removed for access to the items below.

carcase. In either case, strips of wood dadoed into the sides provide simple slides to carry the weight of a drawer.

In essence, a drawer is just a box without a lid and with a sliding mechanism added. I most often make the drawers using a simple mortise-and-tenon technique. The more challenging part is the measuring and accurate routing of drawer guides, both in the drawers and in the carcase of the box. I generally make the drawers to the exact size of the opening allowed for it. That way, when I do the final fitting, a bit can be shaved from the sides and either the top or the bottom edges to get the perfect fit and proper clearance for smooth opening.

Divide and Conquer

The easiest way to add utility to a box is to divide up the interior. Dividers allow the interior of a box to be designed to hold and protect small objects such as jewelry, collectibles, and stationery supplies. A lap joint is the simplest way to make dividers.

Besides the ease with which dividers can be made, they also can be removable or even added to an already finished box. On smaller trays, where the lap-joint dividers would take up too much space and the resulting compartments would be too small to use effectively, I use a simple mortised divider that can be routed into the sides of the trays prior to assembly.

Trays

Sliding trays are another easy way to add usefulness to the inside of a box. If you plan the tray before assembly of the box, a simple strip of wood recessed into the sides of the box makes an adequate track and support for the tray. Sliding trays can be lifted clear when additional access is required. Trays that lift automatically with the lid are more complicated and require more careful planning. Hardware is available to make adding a lift tray much easier than designing the mechanism from scratch, but you should purchase the hardware prior to planning the actual dimensions of the box and tray to make certain that the interior of your box will have enough space for the lift to operate.

There are different techniques you can use for making trays for boxes. Cove-cut trays are particularly useful for small objects like paper clips and stamps that would be hard to pick up from the deeper recesses in a conventional tray. You also can make trays using many of the standard joinery techniques. Mortise-and-tenon, hidden spline, and keyed-miter techniques are all useful in making small trays. The trays I use in boxes are essentially small boxes without lids but with the addition of built-in dividers to make them more useful for organizing and protecting small things.

A cove-cut sliding tray works well for holding small items.

Mortise-and-tenon drawers slide on strips recessed into the sides of the box. Start with a tight fit on drawers and then shave them down slightly to provide just the right clearance.

A wide range of linings can be used for boxes, such as craft foam, fabrics, corrugated materials, leather, hand-made papers, and much more. Craft-supply stores are an interesting place to begin shopping for lining materials.

Interior Linings

Lining boxes with beautiful materials protects the items put inside. Box makers often use spray-on flocking as an easy way to obtain quick linings for boxes. I don't associate flocking with the highest quality in box making but use it on boxes with irregular shapes that would make other techniques too difficult. My favorite lining material is Ultrasuede. Although expensive, it's easy to cut to exact shapes using an Olfa rotary cutter. The relatively high cost of Ultrasuede is offset by the ease of its installation. You can simply glue it in place without the need for additional backing material.

Similarly, leather, handmade paper, felt, and other non-woven materials can be used for linings, cut accurately with an Olfa® cutter, and glued in place. Linings such as velvet, velour, and other woven materials that tend to unravel along the edges require more effort to use as lining materials. I use spray adhesive to attach these materials to a cardboard backing before gluing them to the inside of trays and to box bottoms.

Simple Half-Lap Dividers

The easiest way to make half-lap dividers for the interior of a box is by using a dado blade on a table saw. First, set up the dado blade so the width of the cut equals the thickness of the stock. Raise the blade to one-half the height of the stock, and use a stop block to position the cut (**A**). By using stock of different heights, the top edges can be shaped in advance and still meet in an attractive manner at the cross laps. Here the height difference is ³⁄₁₆ in. and the edges were rounded with a ⅛-in. radius bit (**B**). Look for a slightly tight fit prior to sanding so that after the parts are sanded the fit will be just right (**C**).

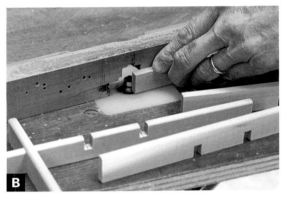

Tray with Dividers

When making small trays, I prefer to use up as little space as possible for the dividers themselves. Using stock as thin as ⅛ in. routed into the tray sides gives the dividers sufficient strength without overly complicating the assembly process.

First, cut the sides of the tray and cut the joints to assemble it. For this tray I used splined miters. Also, cut the groove for the bottom in advance. Lay out the location of the tray dividers on the sides and set up the router table with a 1/8-in. straight bit. These cuts are stopped, so you have to lay the stock down carefully onto the bit. Use stop blocks to determine the length of the cuts (**A**). This task requires concentration as you hold the stock squarely to the fence. I plan the width of the cut so that a single setup will suffice for routing the slots in both the front and back parts of the tray (**B**). During assembly, put the divider parts and bottom in place before gluing the corners together. No glue will be required to secure the dividers (**C**).

Cove-Cut Tray

To make a cove-cut tray, begin by setting up a dado blade or combination blade in a table saw. Clamp an auxiliary fence to the top of the table saw at an angle to the blade. Mark the desired cove on the end of a piece of scrap stock and use that piece for setup. A little trial and error may be needed to determine the right fence angle.

Start with the blade about ¼ in. high, then raise it incrementally about ⅛ in. at a time between cuts until you reach the planned height (**A**). I make the tray much longer than is actually required to allow better control during the cut. Turn the tray end for end between passes to obtain a wider and flatter bottom in the cove. Sand the finished cove cut with a large dowel wrapped with sandpaper (**B**).

To put dividers in the cove tray, use a ³⁄₁₆-in. router bit in the router table and move the tray between stop blocks. You will need to raise the router height gradually to the full height rather than trying to make the full cut in a single pass (**C**). Cut and shape a divider from solid wood and slip it into the slot cut in the cove stock, then glue ends to the cove to finish the tray (**D**). Because these ends are cross-grained to the cove stock, you must use mechanical fastening to give it strength. I use ⅛-in. dowels to strengthen the joint, but brad nails could be used as well.

VARIATION Instead of sanding the tray completely smooth, leave the saw marks in the bottom. The rougher surface makes it easier to pick up small objects like coins and paper clips.

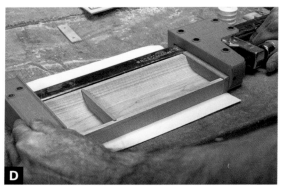

A

B

C

Mortise-and-Tenon Drawers

Mortise-and-tenon drawers begin with the routing of the mortises. Because this particular drawer overlays the sides of the box, the mortise is set in to allow for the drawer front to cover the box sides. The scrap of wood in the foreground was used to test the position of the cutter and stop blocks (**A**).

Set up a straight bit in the router table to cut the tenons (**B**). In routing the tenon, a perfect fit allows the parts to slide easily together but hold with enough friction to defy gravity. Use safety blocking to cover the cutter (here safety blocking has been removed to show the 1¼-in. straight-cut bit for shaping the tenon). Note that the size of the router-table insert is the same diameter as the router bit to give adequate support to the stock during routing (**C**). Move the stock between the cutter and the fence for the cleanest, most accurate cut. Rout a groove in the drawer fronts, backs, and sides for the bottom to fit into. Be sure to use stop blocks to avoid routing through the mortises (**D**).

D

To fit the sides of the box with drawer guides, use the router table and fence to rout grooves in the box sides. I use a ⅜₆-in. straight-cut router bit and again use stop blocks to control the length of the cuts (**E**). Use the same cutter to rout corresponding grooves into the drawer sides. Bump the fence after the first pass slightly widening the cut to allow the drawer to slide comfortably on the guide (**F**). Fitting the drawers to the carcase requires careful measuring and setup of the distance between the cutter and the fence. In boxes with multiple drawers, start at the bottom and work your way to the top, fitting each one carefully before moving to the next (**G**).

Flocked Linings

A quick and easy way to line irregularly shaped boxes is to apply flocking, which is a shredded rayon material that is normally applied with a flocking gun or air-pump sprayer designed to blow the material evenly onto an adhesive-coated surface. Flocking will hide some minor imperfections in the finish.

For small boxes, brush the colored adhesive on the inside surfaces of the box (**A**). Rather than use the spray gun available for flocking large surfaces, I place about a tablespoon of flocking inside the box, close the lid, and shake it until the inside surfaces are adequately coated. This simple approach is far less messy and wasteful of the flocking material (**B**). Empty the remaining flocking material back in the bag for later use, and allow the box to dry before using (**C**).

Woven Linings

Linings from woven materials such as velour and velveteen require that the edges be protected or hemmed to prevent unraveling. An easy way to protect the edges is to affix the material to a piece of backing cardboard or other thin stock and roll the edges to the back side of the material. Thin cardboard like posterboard or cereal packaging will work. I also have used thin Formica scraps where additional stiffening was desirable.

Use spray adhesive to cover the back side of the fabric. My preference is 3-M® Super 77 adhesive. Spraying the whole piece of fabric at once will help to avoid mess. Lay down the cardboard backing pieces on the adhesive-coated fabric, leaving enough material to wrap around the edges (**A**). Using scissors, cut each lining piece (**B**). Cut away the corners to allow for the edges to wrap to the back side without overlapping. Gluing the parts in place will require clamping, particularly where long, slender sides must be attached. It is best to attach the linings before screwing the hinges in place. Use a wood pad to keep the clamps from distorting the fabric (**C**).

Nonwoven Linings

Nonwoven materials can be cut with an Olfa rotary cutter for an efficient, high-quality lining. The secret to accurate cutting is to make a template of the exact size of the interior of the box or tray to be lined. I use Masonite® and carefully fit the template to the space before cutting the material. These materials are difficult to cut accurately using scissors, but a rotary cutter will follow the edges of the template for a perfect fit (**A**). Hold the template firmly over the material and follow around each edge. In thicker material or when using a dull roller, more than one pass may be required (**B**). Use white glue to affix the material to the bottom of the box (**C**).

Hinges and Hardware

Installing Hinges

➤ Mini-Barrel Hinges (p. 114)

➤ Barbed Hinges (p. 115)

➤ Hand-Mortising Butt Hinges (p. 117)

➤ Butt-Hinge Mortises on a Router Table (p. 119)

➤ Quadrant Hinges (p. 120)

Installing Locks

➤ Full-Mortise Lock (p. 121)

Shopmade Hardware

➤ Making Brass Pin Hinges (p. 122)

➤ Making Metal Strap Hinges (p. 123)

➤ Making Wooden Pulls (p. 124)

I F YOU RECEIVE ANY of the major wood-working catalogs, you know that the range of choices in hardware is stagger-ing. The challenge of learning the various installation techniques is enough to keep both amateur and professional woodworkers on their toes. If you are a beginning wood-worker, you may find a sense of excitement in all the choices but also a sense of anxiety about how to accurately install these things in your first boxes.

Choosing the right hardware depends on the size of the box and the quality and price objectives of the box maker. As a bit of research, pay a visit to a gallery, gift store, or craft show and learn hands-on what you like in box hardware.

Choosing Hinges

Hinges are the main hardware item you'll be applying to your boxes. They range from the simplest nail-on brass hinges available at your local hardware store to the finest Brusso® hinges, made to exacting standards for quality work. Hinges that simply nail to the back of a box are the easiest to use and are the most commonly available, but don't trust nails to give the most secure and last-ing attachment, particularly for large boxes. Hinges that mount with screws are generally stronger, and those cut and milled from solid brass rather than formed from brass sheet stock tend to be the strongest and most expensive. They're also most clearly associated with quality workmanship.

> ## ► BOX HARDWARE SAVVY

- Design your box around the available hardware and have the hardware in hand before cutting the first piece of wood. There may be unpleasant surprises lurking in the way hardware fits and functions and the way it will appear on the finished box.
- Make models of the way lid supports will work, so that you can drill holes on the inside of small boxes prior to assembly.
- Do a test fit of hinges and hardware on scrap wood when using hardware for the first time.
- Drill pilot holes and lubricate brass screws with beeswax to help them into the wood more easily without breaking.
- If you can't find the hardware you want, don't be afraid to make your own. I use brass brazing rod from welding suppliers as hidden hinge pins and as jewelry hangers. Wooden hinges are an interesting option; for a rustic look, you can make hinges, latches, and corner irons from scrap steel. One thing for certain, when you make your own hardware, your boxes will be unique.

Lid Supports

Many hinges are made with built-in stops, which eliminate the need for separate lid supports. For example, self-stopping strap hinges and quadrant hinges (shown in the left photo on the facing page) are quite strong but more complicated to install. Butt hinges designed with an integral stopping position are great for small and medium-size boxes where the lids are relatively light in weight. The ease with which they can be installed is an important factor. But these types of hinges are less suited to large boxes, where a separately mounted lid support will give added strength. Lid supports range from simple brass slides that attach to the interior of the box with screws to more complicated supports that require mortising into the box sides. In addition, box lids can be supported with brass chain, leather straps, and any number of shopmade devices, depending on the character of the work.

The Challenge of Brass Screws

Brass is the most common metal used for box hardware, but brass screws are rather fragile and can shear off with unexpected ease. To get a broken screw out may require digging with a chisel, drill, and needle-nose pliers, and the hole left by the extraction has to be filled and redrilled before the hardware can be installed. This is not a rewarding experience. If pilot holes are not marked exactly, you may have trouble getting the front and back edges of the box and lid to align. These problems are common for beginning woodworkers and can be avoided.

Hinges work best and are easiest to fit when they are mortised into the wood on three sides. The mortise prevents inaccuracies in the drilling of pilot holes for the

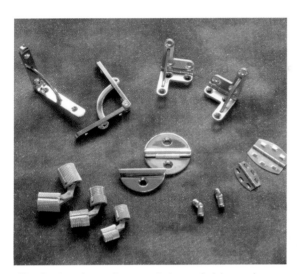

Clockwise from lower right: mini-barrel hinges fit in a 5-mm hole; barrel hinges in 10, 12, and 14 mm sizes; strap hinges with built-in lid support; quadrant hinges; and (at center) round brass hinges with stops.

Clockwise from front: nail-on brass hinges are the easiest to use; Brusso solid-brass butt hinges have built-in stops; drawn brass hinges are strong and light; rolled brass hinges (right) are inexpensive but require mortising.

screws from affecting the way the hinge aligns on the box. Lubricating the screws with wax makes them much easier to screw into hardwood without breaking off. The Vix® bit, which accurately drills pilot holes, is a big help in installing screws both small and large. Also consider using stronger steel screws for the initial hardware installation and the brass screws only for final fitting. This will help you to avoid breaking screws and keep the heads of brass screws from being damaged during installation.

Putting in tiny screws, even with experience, is labor-intensive and demanding work. There's one solution to avoid screws altogether: The small slot or barbed hinges that press in place are so unobtrusive in small boxes that my customers marvel at them. The barbed hinges and mini-barrel hinges that glue in place have made my box making much more efficient without seeming to compromise the quality of the work.

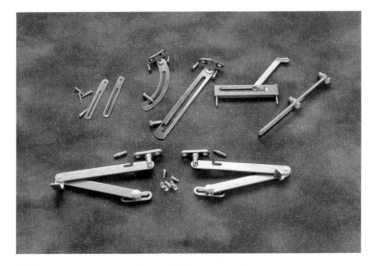

Lid supports come in a wide range of quality, size, and price. Foreground: a brass lid support with a tray lift; in rear from left: two stamped brass supports and two premium Brusso lid supports.

Hinges and Hardware | 109

▶ FLIPPING STORY STICKS

Cutting matching hinge mortises in the base and lid of a box can be challenging. It usually requires a tape measure and marking tools to lay out the precise positions of the hinges, and then chisels, a router, or a combination of both to cut the mortises. In my work, making both one-of-a-kind boxes and small production runs, I've made the process almost foolproof by using story sticks. Traditionally, story sticks have been used by cabinetmakers to record full-size measurements and room features on a job site, then carried back to the shop to serve as guides for making cabinets and other millwork. A simple pencil mark or notch on a length of 1x2 can be as accurate and more useful than the most precise measurement recorded in inches. A story stick requires no math and no fractions.

I frequently use a reversible, or flipping, story stick to set up tools for fitting symmetrical left and right hinges in multiples of a particular box. This technique is easy to understand when used on a drill press but also can be used for setting up stop blocks on a router table and in making jigs to rout hinge mortises. It can even be used to accurately mark hinge positions for those craftsmen who would prefer to do the work the old-fashioned, quiet way—with chisels. In addition, using a story stick to set up tools for box making provides an opportunity to make test cuts without messing up the real work.

The photos at right show making a flipping story stick for installing mini-barrel hinges. First, lay out and drill the right-side hinge holes in both the base and lid of a test box, using the stop block and fence

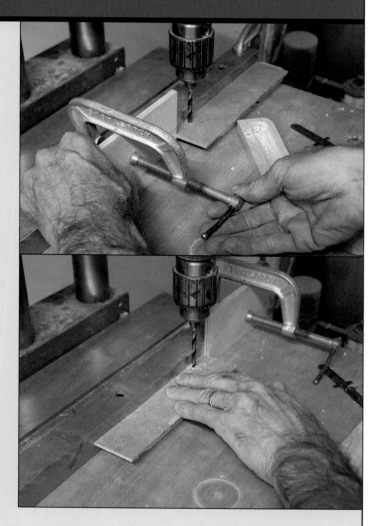

on a drill press to position the parts. Then drill a matching hole through a piece of thin stock using the same setup. That's the story stick. To use the story stick to set the stop for the left-side hinge, simply flip it over and (with the drill press off) lower the bit through the hole. Reposition the stop block on the other side. Keep the story stick for any future boxes with the same hinge and placement.

Tiny Hinges for Small Boxes

On most small boxes, I use barbed hinges, mini-barrel hinges, or brass pins. The barbed hinges are the easiest to install but involve enough complications in setup that make them best suited to production work. I use a ³⁄₆₄-in.-thick Bosch® trim-saw blade assembly mounted in a router table to cut the slots necessary to install barbed hinges. The trim-saw blade assembly is an expensive item for someone wanting to make only a few boxes, but there is no easier way to install these hinges.

Mini-barrel hinges also are easy to use, requiring only a drill press and 5-mm drill bit. The flipping story stick technique (see the sidebar on the facing page) allows you to get the holes in both the lid and box in perfect alignment. This same drilling technique is used for installing barrel hinges in medium and large boxes. Both mini-barrel and barbed hinges require you to cut a 45-degree chamfer at the back edge of the lid and box to allow clearance for opening. This chamfer also eliminates the need for a lid support, as the chamfer provides a resting point for the lid when open.

Another favorite technique for hinging a small box is simply to use a brass pin fitted directly into the wood as a pivot point for the movement of the lid. Brass pin hinges have the advantage of being completely invisible in the finished box. It's also possible to drill for brass pins after the box is assembled.

Butt Hinges

Before the widespread use of the router, installing butt hinges required a marking gauge and chisel. When making a one-of-a-kind box, doing it the old way is more

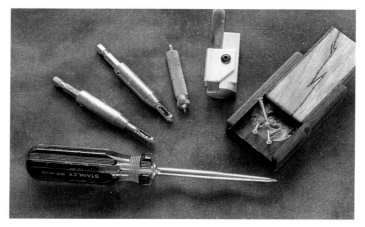

Tools for installing hinges. Clockwise from front: the awl marks the center point for drilling; the Vix bits shown in two sizes drill perfectly centered pilot holes; the center punch helps mark for drilling pilot holes in all but the smallest hinges; corner chisel is used to square the corners of routed hinge mortises; and the box contains wax for lubricating brass screws.

Clockwise from front: a pen box with mini-barrel hinges; an inlaid cherry box (seen from rear) with brass pin hinges; a turned cherry box with barrel hinges; and an inlaid maple box with barbed hinges.

efficient than spending time making router jigs. In my own growth as a woodworker, I moved from cutting hinge mortises the hard way to using the router freehand to remove most of the waste before final chiseling. My next technical improvement involved cutting mortises on the router table. Like most of my other hinge installation work, the flipping story stick is an important part of the process, allowing me to more effectively set up stop blocks for accurate movement of the box along the router-table fence.

Specialty Hinges

Some hinges, like the quadrant hinge from Brusso, can be much more complicated to install than a simple butt hinge and do not really lend themselves to hand installation. I make templates for routing the hinge mor-

tises and the required slots for the support arms to fit. Making templates for use of guide bushings with the router can be a challenge. Some hinge manufacturers such as Brusso also make templates for router installation of their hinges. These are a worthwhile purchase if you plan to use the same size and type of hinge regularly. Whether you make your own templates or buy them, you should use templates on scrap wood before you are tempted to risk messing up the project you are working on.

Locks and Latches

Although locks and latches may not be required on all boxes, they can add a feeling of completeness to certain boxes. Craftsmen working in a more traditional style may want to install a lock to match those used in

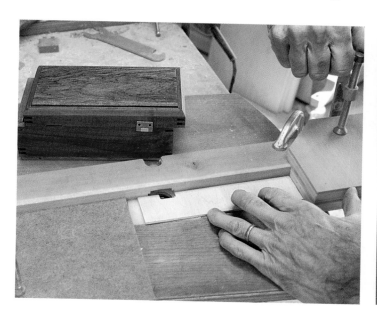

The router table has become my preferred tool for mortising butt hinges, allowing test pieces to be made for accurate fitting without messing up the real box.

Brusso's flat template for routing quadrant hinges is shown at center. The others, with L-shaped clamping wings, are my own templates. They're used in sequence and made in left and right pairs. They all use guide bushings mounted in the router base to control the cut.

Latches and locks for box making. Clockwise from lower right: Brusso solid-brass latches in two types; two common clasps; a simple hook and eye; and full-mortise and half-mortise locks.

The hinges and corner irons shown at left were made from scrap steel banding and brass rod, hammered, and shaped with snips and pliers. The hinges and box shown at right were inspired by the work of British box maker Peter Lloyd.

an earlier era. Common keyed locks come in both full-mortise and half-mortise varieties. The half-mortise locks are difficult to install in a finished box. Full-mortise locks, on the other hand, can be added to an already finished box by using either a plunge router or hand chisels to cut the mortise required for the lock.

Handmade Hardware

I've found a great deal of satisfaction in making both wood and metal hardware in my shop. It is worthwhile to keep your eyes open for other materials that can be used in your box making. Whether using scrap steel for the corners and hinges on a box or making your own hinges from wood, handmade hardware will make your box unique.

Wooden hinges were never a specific interest for me until I saw the work of box maker Peter Lloyd and his expressive and coarsely crafted wooden hinges. Lloyd's hinges made me rethink the qualities that wooden hinges can bring to a box.

There are a wide variety of pulls you can choose from in mail-order catalogs and hardware stores, but I almost always make my

Pulls, both manufactured and shopmade, add to the usefulness of a box. These are left over from a variety of projects. I make more than required and then choose the best, leaving the remains as a reminder for future work or to serve in a pinch for a quick box or two.

own. Most of the pulls I make for boxes are attached to the box using a simple mortise-and-tenon technique. After forming the tenons, I shape the pulls in numerous ways. They range in size from tiny lift tabs for small lids to much more elaborately shaped pulls that require shaping with a template and router.

Mini-Barrel Hinges

The challenge of installing barrel hinges is accurately drilling holes in both the lid and base that align perfectly. A drill press is required for accuracy, and it's helpful to use a stop block and fence to position the workpiece. Set up a fence and stop block on the drill press to drill your first holes (**A**). The depth of the 5-mm hole should be slightly less than one-half the length of the mini-barrel hinge. This will prevent the lid from binding at the back and not closing fully. I use a dial caliper to check the depth.

Use the same setup to drill through a story stick to transfer the position of the stop block for the matching holes.

> See *"Flipping Story Sticks"* on p. 110.

After repositioning the stop block, drill the matching holes. The fence position remains exactly the same for both sets of holes (**B**). Use a 45-degree chamfering bit in the router table to rout clearance for the hinges to operate, then press the hinges in place (**C**). Check carefully that they are oriented in the right direction to bend with the opening of the box. A dab of glue in each hole will help lock the hinges permanently in place.

Barbed Hinges

Barbed hinges press into slots cut in the wood, and the small barbed teeth prevent them from pulling out. For added strength, the hinges also can be glued in place. Installing the hinges requires the use of a trim-saw blade in the router table. Although cutters are made for use on a drill press, the router-table technique allows you to hinge a variety of box sizes with a single setup and gives greater accuracy. I use the Bosch trim-saw blade assembly with a special fence on the router table equipped to remove the sawdust from the operation (**A**).

Always start by using a piece of scrap stock cut to the same dimensions as the box front and back. This allows you to check the position of the hinges, and the test piece will be used as a story stick to position the slots for the opposite side (**B**). Cut the slots in the first set of parts. In this case, the cutter is not quite the correct radius for the size of the hinges, so room is left for the stock to slide about ¼ in. between the stops. Watch for buildup of sawdust that can prevent the stock from moving tightly against the fence or stops (**C**).

(Text continues on p. 116.)

Reposition the stop blocks to cut the slots for the second hinge, then cut the slots. If the base and lid of your box are both the same length, you can rout them all in the same set of operations. In this box, though, the lid fits within the box ends, so I needed to change the location of the stop blocks to rout the lids. Otherwise, the procedure is exactly the same (**D**). Provide clearance for the operation of the lid by routing a 45-degree chamfer on the back edge of the box and lid, then cut a small ledge for the hinge to rest as shown (**E**). Position the hinges in the slots and simply squeeze the base and lid together (**F**).

Hand-Mortising Butt Hinges

There are many times when hand-mortising butt hinges is much faster and more direct than taking the time to make jigs for the router, so it is a technique worth learning even if you prefer to use the router for most operations. As a rule, first mortise the lid, then transfer the location of the mortises to the box directly from the lid.

Lay out the positions of the hinges on the lid using the marking gauge. Set the marking gauge to one-half the thickness of the closed hinge, less a small amount of clearance so the hinge doesn't bind when the box is closed. Mark the edge of the lid (**A**). Adjust the marking gauge to lay out the position of the hinge on the underside of the lid. Remember to allow the hinge to protrude enough for the clearance required for the hinge to open—typically at least one-half of the barrel width (**B**). Using a sharp chisel, make a series of cuts down to the depth of the marking-gauge line visible on the edge of the lid (**C**), then cut in from the edge of the lid to remove the waste (**D**).

(Text continues on p. 118.)

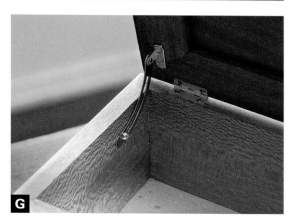

To position the hinges on the base, a favorite trick is to use hot-melt glue. First, tape the hinges in their mortises, spread hot-melt glue on the hinges, and press the lid with hinges in position onto the base. When the lid is removed, the tape will release, leaving the hinges temporarily glued in place for accurate marking (**E**). Use a chisel to mark the position of the hinges on the base, then chisel out the waste to the proper depth. Screw the hinges in place on the box, then attach the lid (**F**). This technique is particularly useful in situations such as this box where the edges of the lid and base are not intended to directly align (**G**).

Butt-Hinge Mortises on a Router Table

Most butt hinges can be mortised easily using a router table. The height of the cutter gives an accurate way to control the depth of the hinge mortise, which determines the amount of clearance between the lid and base. Most router tables are large enough to handle all but the very largest boxes and offer the added bonus of allowing test fittings before you run the risk of damaging your fine work.

Cut a story stick to the exact length of the box. I use thin stock and make the first cut higher than is required to actually mortise the hinge so that it will cut clear through the stock (**A**). The distance between the fence and cutter controls the amount of hinge exposed at the back of the box. To prevent tearout, lower the lid and base directly over the cutter before moving back and forth to rout the mortise. Rout one hinge mortise on both the lid and base at this setting (**B**).

Using the story stick, reposition the stop blocks to cut the second set of mortises. I turn the bit in the router and go as much by feel as by how it looks. The cutter should just barely touch the story stick at the opposite end of its travel (**C**). Rout the second mortise on both the lid and base. Use a chisel to clean up the corners. On larger hinges, you can use a corner chisel, but on these very small hinges, a few quick strokes with a regular chisel do the job. Predrill the holes and wax the brass screws for easy installation. I use an old Yankee spiral screwdriver for small brass screws like this; it provides good leverage but is less likely than a power-drill driver to damage the screw (**D**).

Quadrant Hinges

Because the quadrant hinge offers integral lid support, it is one of the most popular hinges for decorative boxes. It is also one of the most challenging to install. You have to rout a deep, straight mortise for the hinge arm, then rout a shallow mortise for the visible hinge plate itself. Brusso offers an installation template for those who regularly use this hinge. I made my own set of left and right templates. Using either the Brusso template or one of your own allows you to test the fit on scrap wood before you tackle hinging your box.

First, rout the straight, deep mortise for the lid-support arms. This must be done precisely so that enough wood is left for the hinge-attachment screws (**A**). I use a $\frac{7}{16}$-in. guide bushing in a router and a $\frac{3}{16}$-in.-dia. bit. Next, rout the shallow shaped mortises. My template for routing these mortises is designed to use the same $\frac{7}{16}$-in. guide bushing, but with a $\frac{1}{4}$-in. straight-cut router bit. The templates are designed in left and right pairs, each a mirror image of the other (**B**). The finished hinge is strong and attractive (**C**).

Full-Mortise Lock

Installing mortise locks requires careful attention to get a clean fit. Full-mortise locks can be installed on an already finished box, either chiseling by hand or mortising with a plunge router and fence. Both techniques require a bit of careful handwork to get the best results. I drill the holes at the front for the key to fit the lock prior to routing the mortise. Carefully mark and plunge-cut the mortise. Make a series of passes, lowering the bit ¼ in. at a time (**A**).

Using the same cutter and fence setup, rout for the upper catch to fit flush with the mating surface of the lid. Set the depth of the plunge to equal the thickness of the catch plate, then use a chisel to square the cut to fit the catch. This one uses small brass nails to hold it in place (**B**). Next, change cutters in the router to cut for the lock plate to fit. This lock requires a ⁵⁄₁₆-in. cutter. Set the lock in place and mark the start and stop points for the router to travel, then rout between the marks. The depth of the cut should equal the thickness of the face plate (**C**). Install the screws holding the lock in place and attach the keyhole plate (**D**).

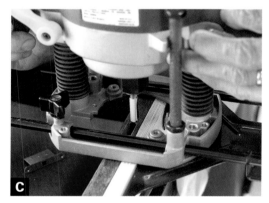

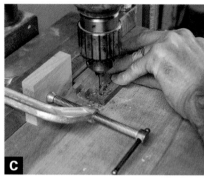

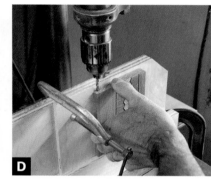

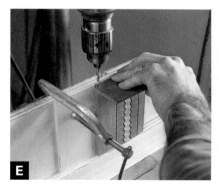

Making Brass Pin Hinges

Brass pin hinges can be used with an already assembled box, but when they are drilled and installed prior to assembly, they are invisible in the finished box. Although they don't offer the option of repair in the event that the box is damaged, they are quite strong for small boxes and fairly easy to use. Get some ⅛-in. or 3⁄16-in. brass brazing rod stock from a welding supplier to make the brass pins. Using an old carbide blade in a table saw, cut the brass stock. You also can use a hacksaw but that takes longer and is harder to get accurate lengths. Cut only partway through the brass stock to keep it from being kicked back by the blade, then break pieces off between cuts (**A**). This will require some trial and error to get the sawblade set to its best height.

Use a drill press to drill the first holes in the ends of the box. I use a 3⁄16-in. drill bit shortened and reground to prevent unnecessary wandering (**B**). Reposition the stop blocks, then drill the holes in the opposite ends (**C**). Using a high fence and stop block on the drill press, drill the pin holes in the lids (**D**). Then transfer the stop block position for drilling the opposite side (**E**). Rout a radius or chamfer along the back edge of the lid to provide clearance for opening (**F**). I use a ¼-in. roundover bit to radius ½-in.-thick lids and position the hinge pins at the center of the radius. Put the pins in place prior to assembly. To make certain that the pins can move freely, apply a bit of wax on the ends as the box is assembled.

VARIATION Drill the holes for the pins after assembling the box. This requires that the lid be held accurately in position with the base during drilling. Use shims (business cards work well) between the base and lid to provide a small amount of clearance when drilling the holes or inserting the pins.

Making Metal Strap Hinges

You can make rustic-looking hinges in your own shop from scrap steel and brass rod. Although the time involved may far exceed the small expense involved in buying hinges, the look of handmade hinges and the pleasure and challenge of the work make them worthwhile.

Use a metal vise to clamp steel banding tightly to round brass stock and begin bending. I often cut the banding narrower to make it easier to bend and to make the hinges appear lighter. As the bend is made, keep rotating the steel stock around the brass until it forms a nearly closed circle (**A**). Squeeze with pliers to finish the job. This part is essential as it tightens the metal banding around the brass stock (**B**). Drill holes for mounting the hinges. Using pliers and tin snips, give additional shape to the hinge parts prior to assembly. I used a ball peen hammer to further distress the metal, making it appear old and hand-forged. Insert the brass rod, then attach the hinges to the box with brass nails (**C**).

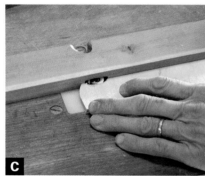

Making Wooden Pulls

I make a variety of pulls from solid wood, ranging from large routed shapes to very small lift tabs on small boxes. All have in common a tenon shaped on the end to allow the pulls to be attached to a mortise routed in the lid of the box. This technique will allow a wide variety of useful pulls to be made from solid wood.

Make a cove cut using a core box bit in a router table. The position of the router-table fence controls the position of the cut. You may feel confident to make this cut by sliding the end grain of the stock along the fence, but adding a backing block of wood behind the workpiece can help to hold the stock square to the fence (**A**). Change to a straight-cut router bit in the router table, and rout both sides of the stock to form a ⅛-in.-thick tenon (**B**).

Make a template for shaping the pull. You can shape the template on a bandsaw, sander, or router table as shown here (**C**). Clamp the template and pull stock together, and use a template-following router bit to shape the pull. Flip the template over to rout the opposite side (**D**). For the final shaping of the pull, use a roundover bit in the router table (**E**). Use a sled on a table saw to cut the pull from the stock, then rout a mortise in the lid for the pull to fit. Installed on a box, the pull can't be mistaken for one bought from a catalog (**F**).

Decorating Boxes

Inlay

➤ Veneer Inlay Strips
(p. 129)

➤ Solid-Wood
Checkerboard Inlay
(p. 131)

➤ Adding Inlay to an
Assembled Box
(p. 132)

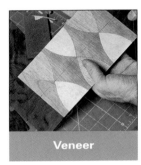

Veneer

➤ Pattern Veneering
(p. 133)

Carving

➤ Chip Carving
(p. 134)

➤ Relief Carving
(p. 135)

THE SIMPLEST BOXES can be beautiful for their function, their shape, or for the character of the woods they're made of. But like an artist standing before an empty canvas and feeling the urge to paint, you'll eventually consider taking the next step and adding some form of embellishment to your work. Three decorative techniques—inlay, veneering, and carving—are associated with the finest levels of workmanship in box making and are thought to represent the highest level of challenge for a craftsman. There's a degree of mystery as a novice wonders, "How did she do that?" and "Is it hard to learn?" Not if you are willing to practice.

Inlay

Inlay and veneering are two closely related ways in which a variety of wood species can be used to add color and design to a box. Whereas veneering is typically applied to the surface of a box, inlay is generally cut into the surface and made level with the surrounding wood. Veneer is often used as inlay material, and most commercially made inlay strips are fabricated from different-colored veneers.

If you study commercial inlay strips, you will notice that they are made from veneers which are layered in stacks, glued, cut into small pieces, and reassembled. This also is a good technique for shopmade inlay. Making inlay strips from veneers works best when

125

A variety of inlaid boxes, clockwise from upper right: simple cherry and maple banding, commercial strip inlay, and shopmade inlays of domestic hardwoods.

Thin veneers form the building blocks for these shopmade inlay strips in a range of patterns.

the veneers are all cut to the same thickness so that equal stacks of different colors and species will build up to the same thickness. I also make patterned inlay from solid hardwoods but at a larger scale. Although they are not as intricate as the strips made from veneers, the color and grain of the specific woods can be more readily recognized.

A variety of inlay strips. The thin ones shown at front are commercially made; the rest I made myself.

Shopmade inlay strips can be a simple piece of wood edged with contrasting woods, or can be assembled from a variety of woods. Typically, bandings are deceptively simple to make and because they are made as a block rather than as individual strips, they take less time than one would first imagine. I make blocks with patterns and then cut thin inlay strips from the block, obtaining a number of inlay strips from a single cutting and gluing operation.

Using a router is the easiest way to install inlay in solid wood. On small boxes, use the router table to rout channels for the inlay to fit. On larger boxes where the fitting of intricate corners may be required, use the plunge router and fence. This requires careful layout of the stopping and starting points for router travel.

Veneering

The use of veneers adds a great deal of creative opportunity to box making, and the way veneers are produced allows special and beautiful woods to be utilized much more

This box made with cherry, bird's-eye maple, burled walnut, and quartersawn oak veneer is built on a substrate of Baltic birch plywood.

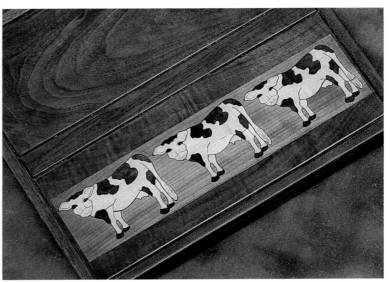

Curly maple and walnut cows grazing on a field of cherry. The cows were cut simultaneously from a stack of different-colored veneers.

efficiently than as thick lumber where most of its beauty is hidden from view. A specialized range of techniques has grown up around the use of veneers, including vacuum lamination and other methods well beyond the scope of this book.

Veneers are generally applied to man-made material substrates rather than to solid wood, so many of the design considerations associated with the expansion and contraction of solid woods can be avoided in the use of veneers. An added benefit is that substrate materials such as Baltic birch plywood and MDF are much less expensive than solid hardwoods. Where veneers are assembled to make pictures, as in the maple and walnut cows shown in the photo at right above, the work is called marquetry.

Veneers can be added to the surface of a box in a solid-colored piece, or they can be cut and mixed and matched to create interesting patterns. Stack cutting is a common technique both for making pictures and for creating geometric designs from veneers; it would be a good starting point for a box maker wanting to learn the process.

Carving

Adding a carved detail to a finished box can be intimidating. After the joints are neatly assembled and I have a great deal of time invested in making the box, I am fearful of messing it up. When I have not carved for a while, I warm up on some practice wood to get the feel of the wood and chisels again. Whether carving free-form shapes or geometric patterns, it is helpful to sketch the patterns directly on the wood, knowing that any remaining pencil lines can be erased and sanded away later.

Basswood is the easiest wood to carve, and its tight, soft grain is resistant to unintended chipout. Most other hardwoods such as cherry, maple, and walnut can be success-

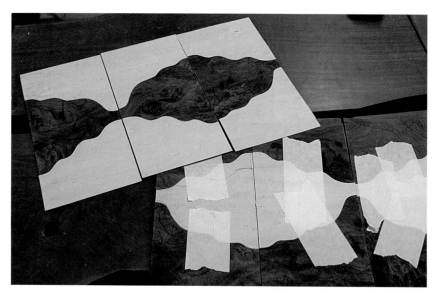

Sheets of different-colored veneers, taped together and cut with a scrollsaw, can yield contrasting patterns.

Two basswood boxes and the tools used to carve them. The box on the left is chip carved. The box on the right shows a simple relief carving.

fully carved, too, but they will require greater pressure with the chisel and more attention to the grain to keep the wood from chipping out unexpectedly. Close-grained woods tend to carve better than open-grained woods.

My experience with carving began as a simple decorative technique to use on furniture, and I have tried to keep my box-carving patterns simple. I usually sketch the patterns directly on the wood in pencil, then with relief carving use cutout paper templates to help in the design.

Chip carving gets its name from the chips removed in creating the design. It has been practiced widely, with nearly every culture having a variation of it. Wayne Barton, one of the world's most famous carvers, does most of his chip carving with just two knives; for the sake of simplicity, that approach can be an excellent starting point. Use a skew knife to stab the wood to remove regularly patterned geometric shapes and a more conventional carving knife for cutting free-form patterns in the wood.

In relief carving, the figure or pattern appears to be raised up from the surface of the box but is accomplished by removing the material in the background. In my own work, I seldom spend much time or attention achieving a perfectly flat background, preferring to leave it textured. Slightly random gouge carving will give the background the appearance of being slightly out of focus and thereby highlight the raised images. Relief carving uses a broader range of knives and chisels, but for simple carving on boxes, a straight chisel, a shallow gouge, a deeper gouge, and a veining tool can do an amazing range of work.

Veneer Inlay Strips

To make inlay strips, begin by layering a couple of different types of veneer with wood glue (**A**). Clamp the sandwich of veneers until the glue is fully dry. Here, I've glued four layers each of walnut and maple, but you can use other arrangements of veneers. Use backing boards to equally distribute the clamping pressure and to keep the veneer sandwich flat (**B**).

Crosscut the veneer sandwich into narrow strips using a toggle clamp to hold the small pieces (**C**). You can make these cuts at 90 degrees, but I made them here with the blade tilted to 30 degrees for a more interesting effect in the final inlay. I then alternated the resulting parallelogram-shaped pieces to contrast the walnut with the maple.

For this inlay, I next crosscut the parallelogram-shaped pieces in half with a 90-degree cut (**D**). Between the resulting pieces I inserted a contrasting segment of cherry. The cherry veneer block was glued up just as the walnut-and-maple block and must be the same thickness. Arrange the inlay pieces for gluing, including a layer of crossbanding veneer on each face of the

(Text continues on p. 130.)

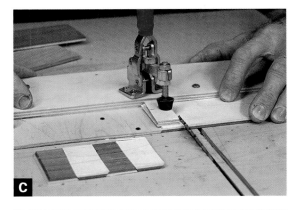

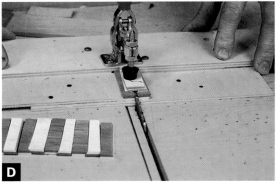

assembly. I used a layer of cherry and one of maple on each side to create the edgebanding. Apply glue to the edges of each piece (**E**). Note the small block screwed to the end of the clamping platform to help keep the parts aligned. Glue the crossbanding veneers, and apply them to the block assembly (**F**). Flip the entire assembly to add the crossbanding to the other side.

Clamp the inlay sandwich securely between cauls, and allow plenty of time for the glue to dry (**G**). Cut the inlay block into thin strips using a scrollsaw or bandsaw with a fence (**H**).

Solid-Wood Checkerboard Inlay

Using a stop block, crosscut strips of walnut and maple into uniform pieces. I use a toggle clamp to hold the small pieces on my table-saw sled (**A**). Alternate the colors of wood.

Spread glue carefully on the end grain of each piece. When assembling and gluing the blocks, use a piece of scrap plywood as a platform. Lay wax paper on the plywood so the blocks don't stick (**B**). Clamp the assembly with a bar clamp, checking the alignment of the parts as the clamp tightens (**C**).

Once the glue has dried, joint one edge and one face of the assembled block so that it will pass easily over the saw, then rip the stock into uniform strips (**D**). For the checkerboard inlay, size the strips the same thickness of the original blocks so that the blocks of the pattern are square. Varying the widths of the strips will yield a different pattern. Arrange the strips in a checkerboard pattern, and glue them together (**E**). I add strips of walnut along the outside of the assembly to frame it. When dry, joint the face of the checkerboard block, then rip off a strip on the table saw to about ³⁄₃₂ in. thick (**F**). You also could saw off the strips on a bandsaw. Rejoint the face before sawing each strip.

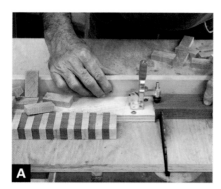
A

B

C

D

E

F

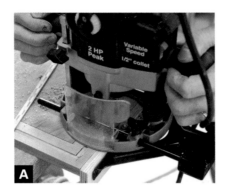

Adding Inlay to an Assembled Box

Set up a plunge router with a fence and a bit sized to the width of the inlay strip. I used a ¼-in. bit to rout for strips nearly ⁵⁄₁₆ in. wide by making two passes and adjusting the fence to fine-tune the width of the cut. At inside corners, mark start and stop points for the router travel. The depth of the groove should be set less than the thickness of the inlay strips so that there will be a little protruding after gluing the strips in. Rout the grooves (**A**), then chisel the corners square and remove the waste (**B**).

Miter the corners of the strips so that they meet in an attractive manner (**C**). Apply a thin bead of glue in the routed recess, spreading it into the corners with your finger. Using blocking to distribute the clamping pressure, clamp the strips in place. I also used strips of Masonite on the back of the lid to prevent marring from the clamps (**D**). Plane or sand the inlay strips down to the level of the surrounding wood (**E**).

VARIATION 1 On a router table, rout the edge of the stock for inlay prior to assembly of the box.

VARIATION 2 Rout the trough for a wide inlay band on a router table, adjusting the fence as required to widen the cut. Use a block plane to shave the edges of the inlay strip to fit the routed channel.

VARIATION 1

VARIATION 2

Pattern Veneering

Make a pattern from ¼-in. Masonite or Baltic birch plywood (**A**). I used a computer to make a pattern, printed it on paper, and then glued the paper to Masonite. The paper allowed me to number each part carefully. Cut the pattern into individual pieces using a scrollsaw. The pieces serve as templates for shaping the veneer.

Next, cut individual pieces of veneer slightly oversize and fix the veneer to the templates using carpet tape. Set up a flush-trimming bit in a router table, and trim the veneer to the template edges. For best results, move the piece clockwise around the cutter (**B**). Arrange the pieces and tape them together with veneer tape or masking tape. Photo **C** shows the down side ready for glue. Check carefully for gaps between the parts before gluing.

VARIATION 1 You can glue curved surfaces using bending plywood with felt padding and heavy rubber bands to hold the stock in place.

VARIATION 2 Assemble the veneers in a sandwich of alternating species. Tape the pieces together, then cut the stack of veneers into pieces on a scrollsaw. Reassemble the parts for applying to the outside of a box.

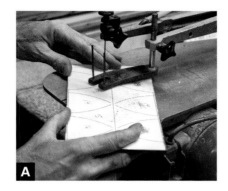

A

B

C

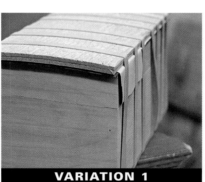

VARIATION 1

VARIATION 2

Chip Carving

Most chip carving can be done with two tools: a skew chisel for cutting geometric shapes and a knife for the curved lines. Lay out your design directly on the wood with a pencil. To transit between the curved edges at the base of my box to the more linear chip carving, I used curved, triangular shapes to fill the spaces. Use the skew to press, or stab, directly into the wood (**A**), then move the chisel into the cut area at a shallow angle to liberate the chip (**B**). When cutting larger triangular shapes, use the skew to stab from the center of the triangle and cut out toward the points. Then with the skew held at a lower angle, cut from the corners along the drawn edges of your pattern (**C**). Cutting free-form on basswood is easier than it looks. Change your body position or rotate the box to gain best control of the cut (**D**). You will get the smoothest cuts if your knife moves in the general direction of the grain (**E**).

Relief Carving

Simple relief carving is used to create designs or figures that appear raised on the surface of the box. You don't need to carve very deeply to give the appearance of depth. Begin by marking in pencil the design on the box. Small templates can be helpful in laying out the general pattern (**A**). Cut the outline of the design into the wood with a straight chisel (**B**), then use a shallow gouge to cut into the outline from the background area (**C**). Using a shallow gouge, remove material from around the raised portions of the carving. Try to keep the cuts uniform in size and depth, yet slightly random in direction; this gives the background the appearance of being out of focus and makes the figure more prominent (**D**). Cut the details into the design using a gouge and veining tool (**E**).

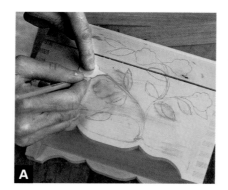

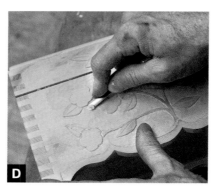

Shaped Boxes

Bentwood Box

➤ Bentwood Box with Carved Lid (p. 140)

Turned Box

➤ Turning a Lidded Box (p. 143)

Bandsawn Box

➤ Bandsawn Box with Drawer (p. 145)

THERE ARE SOME BOX MAKERS who rebel at the very notion of square corners and thumb their noses at the accurate measuring and fitting of parts. They have no interest whatsoever in finger joints, miters, or dovetails. For these box makers, curves are what catch the eye. Soft, fluid lines warm their hearts, and the tools that give fluid shape to wood, like a band-saw and lathe, are preferred to those tools that cut in straight lines. Shaped boxes can be made with fewer tools, requiring less space, and yet be a fully rewarding creative experience.

Bentwood Boxes

Before power saws and routers, making boxes was a low-tech process requiring moderate skill and little else. Bentwood boxes are one of the earliest forms in the box-making tradition. In the United States,

My great-grandmother brought this bentwood box from Norway in 1864 when she was 11. It was split from green wood, planed approximately to uniform thickness, bent after boiling or steaming, and painted in the Norwegian rosemaling technique. At one time, it had wooden latches to secure the lid.

we are most likely to associate bentwood boxes with the Shakers. But many world cultures have had some variation of the bentwood box long before Shaker communities were founded. My great-grandmother, at age 11 in 1864, carried a tine, or cheese box, from Norway to her new home in America. Its simple construction was stout enough to carry her few precious things and then serve my mother's family as an expression of Grandmother Bretha's legacy.

Bentwood boxes can be made by boiling or steaming thin wood and then bending it around a form to obtain a round or oval shape. Where precision is not required, bentwood boxes can be made without a form. The joinery is simple—the ends of the bent sides are laced or cinch-nailed together, and a solid-wood bottom is fit within the cylindrical form. Straight-grained green wood is best for bending. Knowing exactly how thin the wood needs to be is a judgment call at best, requiring some experimentation. Some species of wood will bend without splitting more easily than others, and the tighter the radius of the bend, the thinner the wood must be. A metal cleat attached to the form holds one end of the stock in place as the bend is made. The other end of the stock is pulled around and clamped to the form.

Lathe-Turned Boxes

The lathe is perhaps the most complete tool in the woodshop, allowing you to go from rough wood to a finished box with no measuring beyond the use of a caliper for the fitting of the lid. It is easy to see how turning can become addictive. It is a satisfying experience to watch the chips fly and the shapes emerge.

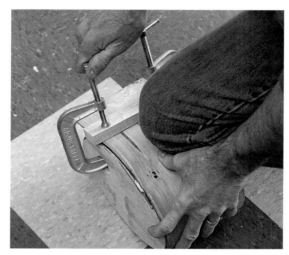

Bending ⅛-in.-thick elm around a form may involve your whole body. The wood was softened before bending by immersing it in boiling water in the bathtub—a good solution in a pinch, but a steam box is recommended for regular bentwood box making.

A turned "satellite" of curly maple (left) and an acorn box of walnut and white oak. Turning works best for small boxes.

The center screw in the Super Nova chuck allows turning stock to be mounted on the lathe for initial roughing out. The hole will be cut away in the final shaping of the box.

The dovetail-shaped jaws of a Super Nova chuck hold the rough stock for a box firmly on the lathe.

A Super Nova chuck grips the inside of a lid for final shaping, sanding, and finishing.

Turning involves the development of specific hand-eye coordination and some knowledge of what each chisel is best used for. Before attempting to make a turned box, you will want to learn and practice some basic turning techniques. One of the favorite subjects discussed by woodturners is how to effectively and safely hold wood on the lathe for turning. My favorite for turning boxes is to use a chuck. Most lathe chucks have dovetailed jaws that can hold the wood either by tightening onto the outside of the stock or by expanding into a turned recess.

The chuck allows you to easily shape both the interior and exterior of a turned box. In addition, chucks are designed to hold a large screw for the initial mounting of rough stock. The screw permits the turner first to shape the outside of the box and form a dovetailed recess at the bottom so that it can be held on the lathe accurately for the various steps in turning a box. Using a chuck allows the box bottom to be removed while the lid is turned and fitted and then replaced for final shaping while it is attached to the box. In addition, the chuck can be opened in the hollowed area of a box and used to hold the lid or base for further turning.

Bandsawn Boxes

Bandsawn boxes are popular, with their drawers and compartments sawn from a block of solid wood. They present a mystery at first: "How was the cut made to form the inside of the box?" Look closely and you'll find a fine line where the first cut was made. In making a bandsawn box, you simply cut wood apart and then glue it back together, with some parts left out. They are easier to make than they may look. The challenge is to decide on the order for cutting. Both lathe-turned boxes and bandsawn boxes require either large pieces of solid wood or pieces glued up from thinner stock. You will need a fine-cutting blade for your bandsaw, ¼ in. or smaller, to make the tight radius cuts required for making a bandsawn box.

Bandsawn boxes from walnut and spalted maple. A bandsawn box is a good way to use that scrap chunk of beautiful wood.

Bentwood Box with Carved Lid

A

B

This box features wire stitching in place of the traditional cinched brass nails used to bind the ends of the bent wood to the body of the box. The bottom is rabbeted and also extends out beyond the box sides. The lift lid is "carved" using an angle grinder and is held in place with vertical latches attached to the box bottom. You can employ any or all of these features or just make a basic version of the bentwood box.

Plane your bending stock to about ⅛ in. thick or less. The thickness required will depend on the size of the radius and the species of wood being used. Straight-grained wood is less likely to split, and green wood will bend more easily than wood that has already been dried. To make the wood pliable, immerse it in a tub of boiling hot water. Remove it while still hot and wrap it around the form to cool and dry.

To make the form, glue layers of plywood together, then bandsaw the glued-up blank to shape. An iron plate fitted to one side of the form holds one end of the stock securely while you wrap the rest of the stock around the form. Note that the bending form is notched for the iron plate to fit so that it doesn't interfere with a smooth shape (**A**).

Drill holes on each side for C-clamps to hold the end in place after the wood is wrapped around the form. Slip one end of the bending stock under the metal plate, and roll the stock tightly around the form. Apply clamps to help the bending (**B**). Allow the wood to dry fully while held to the form. It will spring back slightly when you release it from the clamps. Cut the "fingers" for attaching the loose end of the bending stock to the body of the box. I use a board in a vise to support the stock while carving the fingers; a piece of scrap wood between the layers prevents cutting the box surface underneath (**C**). Clamp the fingers down to the body of the box, and drill holes for lacing the box ends together. Sketch the arrangement of the holes prior to drilling (**D**). Use copper wire to lace the box ends together (**E**).

To make the bottom, trace around the outside of the box onto the wood for the base. I used a piece of thin wood taped to the pencil to bring the line out beyond the box sides by about ⅜ in. (**F**). Cut the box bottom to shape on the bandsaw. Use a ½-in. rabbeting bit in the router to shape the bottom to fit within the sides of the box, then mark with a pencil for hand-chiseling the balance of the stock (**G**). Chisel down along the marked line, and cut in from the edge to remove the waste (**H**).

(Text continues on p. 142.)

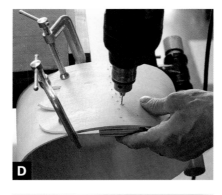

Shape the parts for the latches as shown (**I**). The top piece in the photo shows a shallow dado and saw kerf made on a table saw, while the bottom piece shows bandsawn cuts shaping the upper portion of the latch. The sweeping arc shape allows the latch to bend in use (**I**). Mark the locations for the latches, and chisel mortises for them in the bottom of the box (**J**). Drill holes for ⅛-in. dowels to attach the base to the sides of the box, and hammer the dowels in place. At the same time, position the latches in their mortises, and drill dowel holes through the sides and latches and into the box bottom. Insert all the dowels and trim them flush with the sides (**K**). Cut the lid to fit the catches in their open positions, then use a grinder with a coarse sanding disk to give additional shape to the lid (**L**). The finished box shows a traditional form with whimsical features (**M**).

Turning a Lidded Box

I use a Super Nova chuck to hold stock on the lathe. Drill a hole in the turning stock and twist it into place on the chuck screw. The drawing shows how the depth of the hole limits the thickness of the final box top and bottom. The hole should be no deeper than the planned interior of the box or lid (**A**). Use a skew chisel to form the dovetail-shaped recess on the bottom of the box. The jaws of the chuck will grip this recess for shaping the rest of the box. Next, shape the bottom and lower side of the box (**B**). Remove the stock from the screw, and tighten the jaws to expand in the dovetailed recess. Hollow out the inside of the box, and shape the top portion of the outside (**C**).

Using a skew chisel, form the lip for the lid to fit (**D**). You also can do all the finish shaping and sanding of the inside and top of the box at this point. Mount the lid blank onto the chuck screw with the inside of the top against the screw. Form the dovetail shape on the outside of the lid for mounting on the jaws of the chuck, then begin shaping the interior of the lid.

(Text continues on p. 144.)

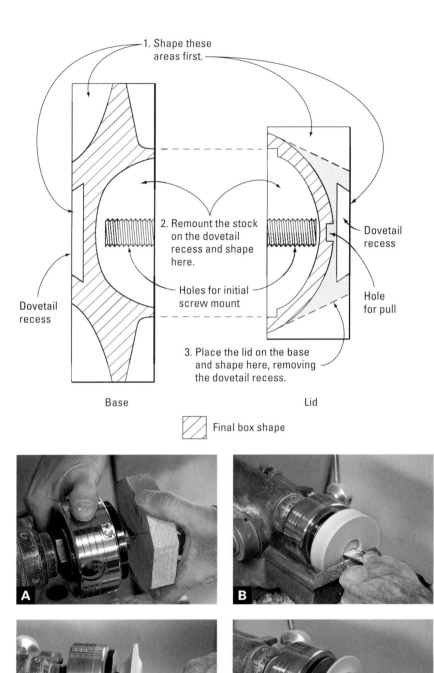

1. Shape these areas first.

2. Remount the stock on the dovetail recess and shape here.

Holes for initial screw mount

Dovetail recess

Dovetail recess

Hole for pull

3. Place the lid on the base and shape here, removing the dovetail recess.

Base

Lid

Final box shape

E

F

Using calipers, transfer the outside diameter of the opening of the box to the lid to determine the inside dimension of the lid (**E**). Use the base of the box to check the fit of the lid. Any small adjustments of fit can be made now or later during final sanding of the base. I prefer a tight fit at this point so that the lid will stay attached to the base during final shaping and sanding (**F**). Remove the lid from the chuck and remount the base. Then, with the lid pressed into place on the base, do the final shaping and sanding of the lid. Note that the dovetailed recess previously used to hold the lid to the chuck is now removed (**G**). If you plan to put a pull or ornament on the top of the box, use a skew chisel to cut a mortise for it (**H**).

G

H

Bandsawn Box with Drawer

This bandsawn box has a top lidded compartment as well as a bottom drawer. The drawing at right depicts graphically the same sequence of cuts and glue-ups shown in the photos on pp.146–147. Start with a block of wood that has been squared on two sides to pass across the bandsaw table and along the fence smoothly and safely. If necessary, glue up thinner stock to get the starting block.

(Text continues on p. 146.)

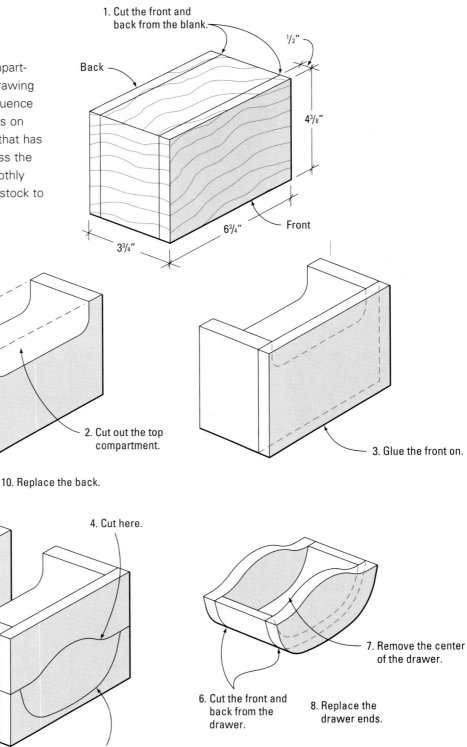

1. Cut the front and back from the blank.

Back

Front

$\frac{1}{2}$"

$4\frac{3}{8}$"

$6\frac{3}{4}$"

$3\frac{3}{4}$"

$1\frac{1}{4}$"

2. Cut out the top compartment.

3. Glue the front on.

10. Replace the back.

4. Cut here.

7. Remove the center of the drawer.

6. Cut the front and back from the drawer.

8. Replace the drawer ends.

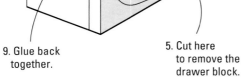

9. Glue back together.

5. Cut here to remove the drawer block.

Take slices, approximately ½ in. thick, from the front and back of the box on the bandsaw (**A**). On heavily patterned wood like this spalted maple, it may be obvious how the wood fits back together, but on less figured woods, add pencil marks to help in the reassembly. Make a bandsaw cut at the top of the box to form the upper compartment (**B**). Before cutting the drawer on the front of the box, glue the front back in place on the block of wood (**C**). Next, make cuts to define the shape of the drawer (**D, E**). Take the drawer block, use the bandsaw with the fence to remove both the front and back, then remove the interior from the drawer (**F**). Glue and clamp together both the box itself and the parts of the

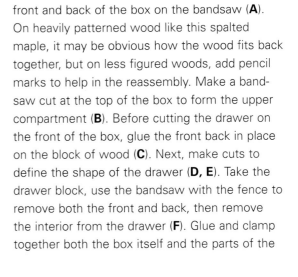

drawer, restoring their shape but with the hollowed spaces remaining (**G**).

Finally, glue the back onto the box (**H**). You can do additional shaping on the bandsaw at this time (**I**). Using a stationary belt sander, remove bandsaw marks from the outside of the box (**J**). Other parts like a base or lid can be added. To add an overlapping base or lid, use a pencil with a block taped to it to trace the shape for bandsawing and routing (**K**). I added a contrasting walnut lid and base to this box (**L**).

Index